NATURAL WITCHCRAFT

NATURAL
WITCHCRAFT

The Timeless Arts and Crafts
of the Country Witch

MARIAN GREEN

Thorsons

Thorsons

An Imprint of HarperCollins*Publishers*

77–85 Fulham Palace Road

Hammersmith, London W6 8JB

The Thorsons website address is: www.thorsons.com

and *Thorsons*

are trademarks of

HarperCollins*Publishers* Ltd

Published by Thorsons 2001

10 9 8 7 6 5 4 3 2 1

A catalogue record for this book
is available from the British Library

ISBN 0 00 712021 4

Printed and bound in Great Britain by
Creative Print and Design (Wales), Ebbw Vale

This book is dedicated to four great 'D's:

Dora S, my mother, who taught me to understand the powers of nature, and died at the age of 93 while I was writing this book;

Dick S, my long-time companion with whom I shared the magical ways, until his death in April 2000. He was a wiccan and a member of Gerald Gardner's own coven, and though our paths differed, we honoured each others' convictions;

Doreen V, with whom I was fortunate to learn some of the arts and skills of the witches, not least the arts of ritual poetry;

Diana D, whose spirit has guided my writing through the winding ways of the old village witchcrafts.

May they all rest in the arms of Mother Earth.

CONTENTS

INTRODUCTION

I have wandered where the cuckoo fills the woodlands

    with her magic voice:

I have wandered on the brows of the hills where the last

    heavenward larks rejoice:

Far I have wandered by the wave, by shadowy pool

    and swaying stream,

But I have never found the grave of him who made me a

    wandering dream.

Fiona MacLeod, 'The Last Fay', from *Poems and Dramas*

Witchcraft is an ancient collection of techniques, arts and crafts of mind and hand, often combined with a deep but personal Nature spirituality. It is not necessarily a group activity, for many individual witches, both men and women, have served their communities as herbalists, healers, midwives, vets and psychologists. They have mended broken hearts, advised on all manner of practical matters, and seen the future through scrying or clairvoyance. Now there are a number of options which newcomers to this esoteric study can take. They can seek out a coven and, after proving themselves compatible to that particular group, its High Priestess and High Priest, and the tradition, be initiated into a coven. Others seek a wilder, more natural path, which may be followed alone, or with friends or relatives, which acknowledges the power of Mother Earth simply and without elaborate ceremony, and which seeks to open up the individuals' own abilities in magic. There are quite a few detailed books on the working of modern wiccan covens but this work mainly addresses older arts and skills of the country witches and their Craft.

Today, because of a growing interest in the arts of magic and witchcraft, all sorts of writers are bringing out fascinating books on the rituals, the spells and the covens of contemporary 'wicca', but some are overlooking the really ancient Crafts and folk magics for which the wise people of old were well known. Historically, there have always been spell weavers, diviners and fortune tellers, healers and herbalists, workers of magic and brewers of potions. There haven't always been covens, high priestesses, athames and festivals on fixed dates all over the world. Certainly that is a path which may suit many modern followers, but this book is mainly about the simpler, more country-based arts and skills, which draw on the oldest association of humanity with the land we live on, with the seasons, the movements of the Moon and Sun, and the sea's tides.

Witches, who were and are both women and men, have always drawn on the powers of Nature to make their magic work. What they believed, the details of their philosophy, the subject of their prayers and invocations will have to be discovered individually by witches for themselves, based on their own world views and personal beliefs. Witches did use herbs and plants and trees to heal, and drew on the resources around them for useful materials and to create charms and spells. They have watched the Moon and the Sun and drawn on their changing light to enhance their work, but in their own ages, have read books, experimented, improved old skills and discovered new ways of dealing with everyday problems.

The opinions and views expressed here are all my own, arrived at after nearly forty years directly involved with the practices of folk magic, witchcraft and ceremonial occult rituals. I have been privileged to be admitted to the hidden circles, the esoteric lodges and the traditional, psychic families by blood and by adoption. However, the ideas expressed here are arrived at from personal experience, long meditation and direct communication with the powers of the land's gods. Although I am bound to never put some old knowledge into writing, there are ideas and concepts which are being over-looked in the witches' new world of the twenty-first century. This book is aimed at helping anyone reconnect with these important sources of power, and find ways of bringing helpful, natural magic into their lives, whether they live in a town or in the countryside.

'Wicca', founded in Great Britain, is an original approach to religion. Part of this work is aimed at showing how, from the 1940s to the present day, 'Wicca' has been built up as a new dimension of 'paganism', a faith which honours Nature, not only as the living world, but also as Mother Nature the great Goddess and her consort, the Horned God or Lord of Wild Things. This new spirituality has been fuelled by the decline of organized religions, which have been seen as too orthodox, too monotheistic and too paternal in a world of equal opportunities for women and men in everyday life. Seekers of a new religious direction acknowledged the lack of a female energy to counterbal-ance the 'God the Father and only God' line of the great faiths, and sought inspiration in the older, pagan religions of Egypt, Greece and Rome, blend-ing in aspects of other multi-deity beliefs. These modern 'pagan wiccans' are not necessarily followers of an old religion, but the heralds of a new one.

There are many ancient arts and crafts, based on traditional skills, which show answers to modern life's problems, and bring health and strength to anyone who is willing to learn them. They are simple, they are safe, and they do not require lots of expensive or strange equipment. The most magical thing any person has is their own mind, and when it is trained to recognize signs and symbols, energies and seasons, a lot of personal power can be made available. The sources of information you might need are far more likely to be illustrated guides to local plants and trees than expensive lists of rituals which use all sorts of equipment, statues and instruments. Why should you need an image of the Goddess of the Moon when she is shining in through your window at night? Why should you have to pay a lot for imported arte-facts when you can make far better ones with your own hands from local plants?

Much real magic is connected to the land you live in and the way the sea-sons change. The traditional festivals and their symbols will vary from place to place, and country to country. You can't have a barley festival if you don't grow barley, or an olive or grape pressing unless these are local produce, so you have to make your own preparations. Some celebrations are worldwide, like full and new moons, but equinoxes are reversed in the two hemispheres, and Christmas is celebrated in mid-summer in Australia and mid-winter in Europe.

When a festival date comes round you must choose what symbols you will put on your altar, what special foods to prepare, what traditional songs or processions you will share. Because many modern pagans worship old gods and goddesses these beings all have their holy or holidays which you can read about, but you can develop your own special rites to mark your birthday, your wedding anniversary or even the death of a loved one. Make your circle, set out your altar, welcome the powers of the quarters, tell the story of the occasion, work the magic or share the feast of the season, and celebrate with ritual, songs, dance and candlelight. No one can dictate exactly how anyone anywhere in the world should hold their festivals because too much depends on local needs and harvests. As your own magic develops, so will your skill in planning and enacting powerful rituals or feasts.

One

MOTHER NATURE'S CHILDREN

'They are the children of one mother, she that is called Longing,

Desire, Love' one told me; and another 'Her secret name is

Wisdom'; and another, 'they are not three but one.' And another

'touch them not, seek them not, they are wind and flame.'

I have come back from the hidden, silent lands of Faery,

and have forgotten the music of its ancient streams;

Now flame and wind and the long, grey wandering wave,

and beauty and peace and sorrow are dreams within dreams.

Fiona MacLeod, 'Dreams within Dreams', from *Poems and Dramas*

We are all the children of Earth, from whose storehouse we get our food, maybe processed and bought in a supermarket now, but grown in the earth, fed with rain, and strengthened by sunshine. Our cycles of sleep and waking are ruled by the cycles of night and day, our dreams are influenced by the light of the moon, and our health by the warmth of the sun. The clothes we wear may be grown as cotton, or linen from flax, or coloured with plant dyes. Our houses have the wood of trees used in furniture, our computers are made of plastics which come from oil-based materials, and the silicon chips in our computers are minerals. Everything we have came from the earth, which originally came from the stars, so everything in the cosmos is linked. These links allow the changes, which may be called magic, to happen. By learning about these natural things we can find ways to transform them to make our world a better place. It is necessary to be able to sense things beyond normal awareness through observation and clear sight. It is also important to respect other people, places and even plants and their powers, and to try to live in harmony with Nature.

Although few of us who try to follow the old ways now make our living entirely from the land, the sky above our cities still contains the same stars and planets, though seen more dimly through the street light glare; we still suffer the same weather with its droughts and deluges as those in more rural places. Our gardens and parks show the same changes of growth of new leaves in spring and their fall in autumn as is seen in forests and farmland. It may be harder for us to link in with these essential and real energies which power the life-giving current which turns the barren fields to green, and then to gold at harvest time, but it is possible, if we are willing to make the effort.

We may live in the same world as that of our ancestors, under the same sky, and eat the same foods and feel the same wind and rain, but they would recognize very few of the things we have around us, and take for granted. They would be amazed at the uses of electric power, the speed of cars, and the way we control the environment. If we found ourselves transported to the past we would probably be helpless and uncomfortable in a world without all the comforts of a draught-proof house, clean-running water, instant light, convenient shops, appropriate clothes and the thousands of things we use all the time. It is easy for us to forget that these inventions have mostly come into being in the last hundred or so years. We may still have the same curiosity about the meaning of life, a desire for magic, and a yearning for the old ways, but our world is really very new. So are some of the ideas which interest people today.

The practice of Witchcraft is continuing to spread, mainly through the innate fascination of young people in magic, mystery, the occult and the supernatural. This is fuelled by recent popular novels, endless TV shows and films, articles in the press and serious academic books. Many of these may be works of fiction, or have special effects which intrigue viewers, but most people recognize that underneath the Hollywood gloss, the publishers' hype and the sensational presentation in newspapers, there are ancient stories being retold. Stories which contain seeds of truth, based on ancient myths, folk tales and legends, where heroes and heroines succeed against all the odds, where mystical powers of light fight those of darkness, and where ordinary people triumph, sometimes with supernatural help. And even in the twenty-first century witches, wizards and magicians are alive and well and probably living in a city near you.

Some of us know that these inner seeds are true, that magic is real, that we can return from death into a new incarnation, or speak with beings unseen to the everyday eye, be they mythical beasts, angels, elves or spirits of the land. That is what the old Craft is about. It teaches that, even as we live in the mundane world, all around us are aspects of the otherworld, powers offering help, and inner strengths which every individual can call upon. We know about these things, not because we read about them in a book or saw a programme on them, but because we have learned to cross the twilight bridge which separates the known from the unknown into the land of dream. There is a vast region of this landscape of the mind where anyone can learn to roam, and where the true and ancient roots of witchcraft have their ancestral home.

This is a quite different path from the coven-based, hierarchical, structured and book-bound ideas of wicca. The old magics are wild and free, they can only be encountered when the heart is unbound to sense, and the eyes are open to the hidden realms. The tracks of the old witches wound through the realms of night and day, recognizing the healing and illuminating powers of plants, knowing the sacred in stone and tree and curve of a river. Today more and more rules are being printed in books, limiting wiccans to fixed dates, house-bound circles and convenient times rather than encouraging seekers to wander under the great and sacred circle of the sky, at times when the great forces which they perceive as Gods and Goddesses offer the guidance they need.

Some new followers of the old ways are being diverted into a new cult of pre-written rituals, with stage directions, props and scripts, so they appear more like amateur dramatics than heartfelt, natural wisdom and spirituality evoked by the very ground we stand upon. A great deal of stress is being laid on 'pagan' beliefs, worship of ancient Gods and Goddesses, often quite alien to the land where the newcomers are living. It is impossible to prove what any witches thought or believed hundreds of years ago. It is very likely that they had original and possibly unconventional views, but these were never brought out into the open, no one was accused of being a pagan priestess in any of the trials, or of worshipping Classical Gods, and there is no hint of anyone even acknowledging a Goddess anywhere in the accounts of the investigations by the Inquisition. Any of those ideas would have been headlines in their day, and they would have been recorded with comments in the court papers of the time, but they have not been discovered.

If you are willing to put aside, just for a moment, the idea that old witches worshipped the Gods of ancient Egypt or anywhere else, how is it possible to say what they may have believed or honoured? Witchcraft was always about magic which some people in authority found unsettling and uncontrollable. It was about making changes by healing, by seeing into the past or at a distance, by understanding the tides and cycles of the land, and probably by keeping mental records of who was related to whom. Any child who has come across fairy stories would be able to tell you that witches could fly on broomsticks, make potions to heal illness, curse people, tell fortunes and talk to animals. How many still do today? Quite a lot, in fact, especially the country witches who have had little time for the new teachings, initiations and degrees, priesthoods and ceremonial scripts.

Their relationship has been to the land they live on, whether it is a city, a town or a remote farm, to the natural cycles of the Moon and the Sun, to the seasons and the wisdom inherited from their ancestral line. Not all are children of witches, though in some families there has been a long heritage of healing abilities, power to see the future, and knowledge of how to perform spells or lead festivals. Each one of us has inherited parts of our genetic make-up from thousands of forebears, some will have had extra skills, just as some people are naturally musical or talented at sports or creative art. Until recently no one inherited computer genius, but many have mastered this and other new technologies and managed without a genetic propensity for that skill. The same is true of magic.

Yes, it does help to have psychic ancestors because it is quite hard to learn to be sensitive from scratch, but that isn't essential. It helps to have had someone around when you were young who taught you the names of wild plants and birds, and how to tell what the weather would be, but it is not vital. It helps to have been able to run freely across unpolluted fields, explore woods, learn that the darkness of night is nothing to fear, and to be able to see and recognize the planets and stars, the phases of the moon, and the seasons. It is good to have an understanding of the lives of animals, both domestic and wild, knowing where your food comes from, how it is produced, and better if you can prepare it yourself. What is essential is the acceptance that we are part of the web of living things, that our lives change those of plants, animals and microbes. What we have to understand is how to do this as lightly as possible.

Humans are happy destroying the planet, assisting global warming, using up precious and irreplaceable resources, burning the odd candle (and enlarging the hole in the ozone layer, because paraffin wax is derived from petrol), and chanting to the Moon to heal the Earth at the same time. Good, isn't it? Every single person who considers her- or himself to be a witch should seriously examine what they really believe deep down, what they are doing and the effects it will have on the rest of the planet. It is no good pleading ignorance, nor can anyone really prove that they are doing more good than harm to this world we all share. If we do not act *this minute* to try to undo the harm we as a species has done to our home, we won't be here to enjoy it forever. We only have one planet, we only have one set of resources, we only live one life at a time when we can act for good or ill, and our acts will affect every other inhabitant on this green globe of ours. We will affect people, animals, plants, the water and air, and even the bacteria by just being alive, and we need to act now to live up to the oft-said but seldom understood, 'An it harm nought, do what you will.'

We need to reassess our relationship with the planet Earth, which is our Mother. She gives us a home, food, water and air, and we can't make up for our destructiveness by saying a few prayers and burning a bit of incense. We have to live in real harmony with Nature, even if it is inconvenient. We need to examine what we really feel about the importance of 'paganism' in our lives. Those who recycle, reuse things, tread lightly on the earth, grow their own herbs or food crops, go out and shoot their own dinners or just eat what each season offers, or draw on supplies they have preserved themselves in lean times, probably won't call themselves pagans, but are they not closer to the original idea? Do we need to pretend we belong to some ancient religion with a book of rules to adhere to, established priesthoods, fixed festivals and all the wooden, rigid structures that free-thinking natural spirituality requires, or can we think and act and believe for ourselves?

We need to get to know the forces of Nature as they are and not impose our human ideas on what they should look like, when their feasts should be and how they ought to be celebrated. We need to master silence and listen to the wind to teach us the breathing power of inspiration. We need to harken to the voices of the waters to learn to flow and move gently across the land, and when we change or reshape things to do it for the better. We need to observe the bright destroying flames of fire and know that the time for some things has now passed away and that they need to give rise to new ideas, and provide vitalizing ashes for what is to come. We also need to turn inwards and consider what we really think about the Gods and Goddesses in our secret hearts. Do they exist? Do they want to talk to us or offer us teaching? What are they and what are they like? How can we communicate with them? Can they offer us help or we them? What do you really think about these ideas?

The old Craft is about questioning what is actually real around us, and then seeing, if something needs changing, the most gentle, original and effective way of making that change. It means learning what magic is, how its powers may be invoked and controlled, what it costs in human terms, and when to leave well alone. It means finding out who and what the Gods of your homeland are, their names, powers, specialities, likes and dislikes, and then creating a two-way friendship with them. We have no right to command things to go the way we want them if all we are going to do is give orders and sit back, waiting for results.

Each of us needs to forge, through the fires of reality, a new partnership between us, bodies and souls, and the Earth, planet, Mother and foundation of our lives. If we can achieve that, then we have some chance of seeing a new dawn of human life in the years to come. If we are too busy reading books, buying factory-made artefacts, burning candles and chemically-created incense, we won't notice the crises building up around us. The old witches based their skills on observation and awareness of what was actually happening around them, so that they could predict any changes that were in the offing. By knowing this they could seem to be in charge, and use their magic to the best effect. We can do this too, but all of us need to deal with the real world, with all its astral levels in our dreaming minds, not the virtual world invented by others.

It isn't possible to discover unbroken lines of belief, practice or heritage in witchcraft. Although some modern commentators would like there to be a clear link with the priesthoods of the pagan gods of classical times, no such connections can be discovered or proved. We can see, largely because the factual evidence exists in writing, in museums, in private collections, and often in the memories of people still living, who were there at the time! Certain recent ideas became blended with earlier developments in religious freedom, psychology and social structure to create a seedbed in which this new pagan religion was to grow. We shall examine some of the factors which led to the enormous upsurge of interest in and the practice of varieties of witchcraft, set out in far greater depth in a number of recent books, often written by 'insiders'.

First we must look at the modern developments in both the arts and crafts of witchcraft and the more coven-orientated and pagan 'wicca'. There are all sorts of reasons given for the increase in interest in witchcraft and paganism in the 1950s, and some commentators imagine that it was a sudden re-emergence into the light of a truly ancient religion which had been repressed for thousands of years, released at last, in Britain, by the repeal of the Witchcraft Act in 1951. Certainly some of the people who began to write books on the Craft from the inside, had their works published after World War II, and this trend has gradually expanded since then. But the interest in the occult, in magic and witchcraft, is both a very old part of human philosophy and also a very modern practice.

Although Gerald Gardner and others did start to write books in the 1940s which have spelled out the prayers, festivals and practices of wicca, they were adding a chapter to a development of new spirituality which began in the 1800s. During the nineteenth century, people in Britain and much of Europe lived in a very structured society, where everyone knew their position in the world. During the 1700s many people had left their homes on farms and in the countryside to move to the great towns and cities where they could work in factories. With the development of canals to transport goods, and then the railways which permitted people to move around much more, the whole patterns of life changed.

Into this materialistic setting came the poets, the novelists and writers, and later the magicians with their visions of a lost Golden Age. Scholars began to yearn for perfect country idylls, they longed for the eras when the ancient gods roamed the earth befriending shepherds and country girls, and peace and beauty were all around. Poets wrote new prayers to ancient goddesses, and the stories of ancient Greece and Rome reappeared in opera and song. Pre-Raphaelite artists painted legendary scenes, setting contemporary models in ancient landscapes or temples, surrounded by mythical creatures and the deities of the Classical world. A whole body or artistic creation based on romance and mythology was made available to ordinary people, all over Europe.

Whole movements of philosophy, arts and crafts tried to hark back to simpler, more rustic times, when things of beauty were made by hand, and toil on the land was valued. Romantic poets invoked the Great God Pan in verse and playwrights recalled times long gone. Although the church was important as a kind of cement in society, uniting rich and poor in largely protestant worship, there was an undercurrent among the intelligentsia favouring the gods of the past. On the whole these were seen as symbols of fertility and power, of ecstasy and freedom, rather than a new or old religious impulse. People wanted the symbol rather than the reality then just as much as we do today. Into this romantic era came a new magical current too, as part of the use of ritual in secret societies, the search for forgotten knowledge and discoveries like the Tomb of Tutankhamun.

Other thinkers studied folk customs and old traditions, often giving them meanings which were quite alien to those of the people whose ancestors had been performing them for generations. They sought magic and mystery in common country feasts. By the end of the 1800s there was a vast amount of attempted understanding, reinterpretation and pure guesswork applied to the past. Some wrote learned papers, re-invented Druidism, turned masonry from a skilled art of stone cutting into a speculative and philosophical system for men who had never attempted to shape rock, and established a whole, largely fictional reinterpretation of history.

In the eighteenth century, landowners and educated people began to take an interest in relics of the past, especially the great earth mounds, the standing stones and rings and the other ancient monuments all around them. They dug open burial mounds, looking for treasure, and tried with what limited resources they had to decipher their history, and to understand who had put up these stones and barrows. Often they believed that the Romans were responsible because they had no way of knowing the abilities of people from the Stone Age. It has only been since the introduction of scientific archaeology that the true age, manner of construction and probable use of the ancient monuments has started to emerge. Even today there are still questions and mysteries left by our many-layered heritage from the inhabitants of the past.

One of the hardest puzzles to unravel is, why did the people who built vast stone or earth structures, and later the enduring and beautiful stone of Egypt, Greece and the Roman empire, do it? Were these intended as shrines to the gods of sky and land, monuments to the dead, dwelling places for the immortals, or markers of their battles? Were they universities, parliaments, hospitals, refuges in war, or just markets where people came to trade and exchange produce? We may have some answers, but not all. Even if we are told the uses of these places, we still don't know what the people believed about life and death, whether they had sacred days, if they acknowledged the powers of great gods and goddesses. Long ago something prompted large numbers of people in many parts of the world to work together, freely, or by coercion, to mark out special places whose shapes have endured for thousands of years, but we have no idea why. Lots of writers have speculated, both from known fact and from wild supposition, as to the functions and uses of these places, but *we do not really know*. We can't say, 'Well, they were pagans, worshipping the Sun and the Earth, on the mid-winter solstice,' or any such thing. That would be to guess, but it has happened a lot since the 1950s.

Some interesting themes have gradually come to light, from which a great tree of witchcraft and magic has grown. For example, in 1885 a group of Freemasons came upon some coded documents which, when deciphered, explained the rituals, degree ceremonies, and related knowledge required by members of a Hermetic Order of magicians, based in Germany. The rites were elaborate, and not only involved men but gave women an equal footing in the work, perhaps allowing them to stand at ancient altars for the first time in thousands of years. This knowledge was gradually expanded until a number of lodges were founded all over Great Britain, in France and later America.

From this came developments in the arts and crafts movement, and a widening of participation in magical ritual which was not directly associated with a current religion. The parents needed to create the new Child of Nature had shown themselves, with Art and revived ancient religion on one hand, and the power of hermetic magic on the other. From these were born the new witchcraft movement in the middle of the twentieth century.

Today we are surrounded by information in many forms, but you will have to look back to a time when news was spread mainly through the printed word. The times of electricity in every home, of radio and television and computers, were still far in the future during the first decades of the twentieth century when the infant pagan witchcraft movement was born. For entertainment, people went to theatres or music halls and they lived in a very much more regimented social hierarchy than we do, when quite ordinary people had servants, and motor cars and telephones were just becoming more readily available. In our world of instant everything it is really hard to know what life would have been like, but without making an attempt to understand the social setting, the developments of the re-emergence of magic and witchcraft are hard to comprehend.

Gerald Gardner and Doreen Valiente probably had no idea how much influence the books, prayers and poems they published would have on people in the following half-century. From what must have been explanations of quite personal experiences, whole flocks of new High Priestesses and High Priests have gained enough material to initiate thousands of covens and wiccans all over the world.

Doreen Valiente, who died in September 1999, had no inkling how famous she was, having withdrawn into her own private life of writing books and poetry, seldom appearing in public. Speaking at a Conference in London in 1998 she was amazed that 2,000 people turned up to hear her, and that they gave her a lengthy standing ovation. She believed that she had been forgotten, yet it is the words of her prayer, 'The Charge of the Goddess', which begins 'Listen to the words of the Great Mother ...', which is used in covens world wide. Often those using these beautiful words have no idea that they were written in the 1950s, based loosely on information from an Italian witch in the 1890s.

The man who began to publicize the tradition of pagan witchcraft was a retired civil servant, a researcher and folk historian, not someone with long family links to the land or the traditions of the country folk. This was Gerald Brousseau Gardner, born on 13 June 1884, and his life story has been told in a number of books. His involvement with witchcraft doesn't appear to have occurred until quite late in his life. He had been interested in the history of peoples in the Far East and had written a book about their ceremonial knives, called krisses. His last job was in Malaya, working as a customs official, and he retired to England in 1936, settling first in London. In 1938 he and his wife, Dorathea, usually called Donna, moved to Hampshire, close to the New Forest, and it is there that he claimed he came into contact with real witches, and was admitted to their circle. He wrote that these people had kept alive a fragment of the pre-Christian pagan belief, with festivals, initiations, covens and Priestesses.

Sadly, traces of this surviving tradition of old witchcraft, as Gerald explained it, tend to become more and more elusive the closer you look at them. The people he names as his initiators turn out to have left original diaries and note-books, detailing not naked romps with coven members in the Forest, but accounts of church fetes, gatherings of Conservative party fund raisers, and vicarage tea parties. Although he was involved with the Folk Lore Society in London and discovered a Rosicrucian Theatre, in Christchurch, Hampshire, the main characters of Gardner's version of the survival of an ancient cult don't add up.

Gerald Gardner, after whom the Gardnerian form of witchcraft is named, wrote several novels. One of these was *High Magic's Aid*, which was eventually published in 1949 by the owner of Atlantis, a London bookshop. Gerald Gardner wrote other books on witchcraft as he saw it, or wished it to be, including *Witchcraft Today* and *The Meaning of Witchcraft*. It is from these works that a large part of pagan witchcraft or wicca was created, because he spelled out rituals, named festivals, published scripts for initiation and further degrees, and laid many of the foundations of this new 'old religion'.

Although Gerald probably didn't encounter many traditional witches he was clearly influenced by something to gather these ideas into a working pattern. Taking ideas from Freemasonry and ceremonial magical orders to which he had been admitted, he began to build up a system of three degrees and, helped by more fluent writers than he, gathered poetry, prayers, ideas and ritual forms. One influence was the writing of Aleister Crowley, once dubbed 'the wickedest man in the world' by a Sunday newspaper. Crowley's poetry and his Gnostic Mass, from which some of the words of wiccan ritual are taken, had been published more than twenty years before Gardner borrowed them. There is a brief account in Crowley's diary of his few meetings with Gerald Gardner, which took place in May 1947, shortly before Crowley died in Hastings, later that year. Crowley kept detailed diaries throughout his life, many surviving in historical collections, and these note his activities, the people he met and the rituals he performed. They demonstrate that he was not part of any witchcraft group, and he did not write or design material for what became 'wicca', as has been alleged.

Although Gerald worked with a priestess he called 'Dafo', she too appears to be a pillar of respectability, although local newspapers of the time, around the 1940s and early 1950s, show that Gerald and Dafo were members of a local historical society with plans to set up a museum of Folk Lore in the New Forest. Another plan was to buy land next to a nudist camp in Bricket Wood, Hertfordshire, as Gerald had enjoyed naturism in the Far East as an aid to health. In the end money was put up to buy some land, and erect upon it a small cottage, made as an example of 'a witch's house' from the 1600s for an exhibition of building methods. This is the actual birth place of wicca, it seems. Gerald was not a fluent writer so he and others he worked with began to collect suitable material to construct *The Book of Shadows*, which contained information of coven structure, rituals for each of the eight main festivals, called Sabbats, and the esbats held at each full moon. There was a three-degree system of initiation, similar to that of other 'secret societies' which had flourished since the 1700s. Apart from some of Aleister Crowley's poetry another influence was to be found in a book by Charles Godfrey Leland.

Leland was an American researcher into folklore who wrote several books on his explorations in Italy and one of them, *Aradia, or the Gospel of the Witches*, published in 1899, contains information given to him by an elusive lady called 'Maddelena' who he believed was a witch. She told him of spells, prayers and magical arts, which included poisons and curses, and contacts with fairies, elemental spirits and the Goddess Diana and her brother Lucifer. No one has been able to show that these were real survivals of a long Italian tradition of witchcraft, or if the stories Leland reported were true, but they formed another section of the foundations of wicca when Gerald Gardner got hold of them. It is in this book that witches are encouraged '... as a sign that ye are truly free, ye shall be naked in your rites, men and women also: this shall last until all your oppressors shall be dead.' *Aradia* also contains instructions of how to bless food and drink, conjurations of Diana and of Aradia, who was the daughter of Diana and her brother, Lucifer, details of the Sabbat dances, and various myths of the Goddesses of ancient Italy. Charles Leland was fascinated by the idea of goddesses, and many of these imported ideas were woven into the fabric of the infant wicca.

Once Gerald Gardner got hold of this he began to develop his ideas, helped in the 1950s by Doreen Valiente. He liked the idea of nudity or being 'skyclad' in ritual as a way of enhancing magical power, and though many people imagine that wild sexuality was also part of these rites, in practice most covens consist of established partners, and if they wish to make love as part of their magic, they do so in privacy. Gerald believed that binding with cords and scourging also aid the changes to consciousness needed for spell-weaving, and empower wiccan magic. Historically, scourging was used for religious penance by a Christian brotherhood, the Flagellants, or as punishment of criminals of the worst kind. Many secret societies include blindfolding, being bound with cords and some kind of ritual humiliation including nudity in their initiation ceremonies, and in some wiccan traditions these practices of scourging and binding are part of many rituals as they are thought to increase the potency of the work. Not all groups work skyclad, use scourging even in a symbolic fashion or bind members of their covens, except with oaths of secrecy! Some groups are naked for initiations but wear robes out of doors, others who follow the country witches' path wear ordinary clothes or warm cloaks when greeting the goddess of Earth in her own domain. Today it is possible to use whichever methods you and your group, coven or friends feel most comfortable with, when and how you please. As said before, there really is no one book of rules about this fast-growing new faith.

Other writers whose works influenced the development of wicca include Dr Margaret Murray, a historian and archaeologist. In her very long life she wrote many books, including *The God of the Witches* and *The Witch Cult in Western Europe*, and seemed to believe that there really was a cult of witches who were burned at the stake (although not in England, where they were hanged), who were part of a surviving old faith. She thought that covens were led by a Man in Black and that they worshipped a Horned God, although most modern wiccans give great prominence to various goddesses. Much of her reasoning, based on accounts of Scottish witch trials, is now disputed, and the idea of an unbroken, surviving pagan tradition is considered to be speculation. However, in the 1950s and 1960s her works gave impetus to those who were looking to expand witchcraft as a living religion.

Another influential source was the poet Robert Graves' book *The White Goddess*, which expounds the notion that creative inspiration comes from the White Goddess, found in many ancient cultures. Robert Graves draws on a number of complicated mythic themes, including long Welsh riddling poems which he decodes as information on ancient alphabets and hidden wisdom. It isn't really a guide to a pagan religion, or the stories of actual goddesses, but rather an example of the way in which poets treat information.

He draws all sorts of inspired conclusions which have influenced other writers and pagan thinkers since. He more or less invented the Celtic Tree alphabet, and a whole Celtic divination enterprise, based loosely on the researches of Edward Davies in a book published in about 1800. Again, the historical evidence for a surviving Celtic or ancient British pagan religion is extremely thin on the ground. Probably, if these old faiths had survived they would be very different to their modern interpretations.

Another person who did a lot to publicize his own brand of wicca was Alex Sanders. Although he claimed a long ancestral heritage of the Craft and initiation in childhood, the rituals he produced to his followers in their Books of Shadows is pretty much the same stuff as Gerald Gardner and Doreen Valiente's joint effort. We know that is not particularly ancient, unless a fifty-year-old tradition makes it antique. Sanders drew more on Qabalah and ritual magic for some of his work, and in the late 1960s was involved with an off-shoot of Scientology, called The Process, which ran a cafe in London. He and his followers held rituals and teach-ins there, but he also sought publicity in the newspapers, participating in rituals in public places, and talking on the radio and TV. Two of his initiates, Stewart and Janet Farrar, went on to write many valuable books, including *The Eight Sabbats for Witches* and *The Goddess of the Witches*, among many other titles.

Once there was a collection of characters coming out in public and declaring they were witches, all sorts of others jumped onto the bandwagon. In 1951 the last 'Witchcraft Act' in Britain was repealed, substituting a 'Fraudulent Mediums Act' which allows witchcraft and magic, but bans anyone from 'purporting to tell fortunes for money', which ought to silence everyone from newspaper astrologers to TV psychics. Thirteen years later, in 1964, the editor of a small magazine called *Pentagram* organized a formal dinner, in London, to which pretty well the whole of the witchcraft movement at the time were invited. Doreen Valiente spoke to an audience of about fifty people!

Since that time individuals have come forward to establish covens all over the world. There are traditional witches, hereditary witches, followers of Robert Cochrane and Evan John Jones who, with Doreen Valiente, wrote *Witchcraft: A Tradition Reborn*, and, more recently, hedge witches. In America and other parts of the world, writers and witches who received initiations from British covens gained authority to start their own traditions and variations, and many individuals and groups found other sources to claim as their heritage, some from Europe and some from other forms of native spirituality. As well as the assorted wiccan traditions there are lots of other shades of modern paganism available; including Druidism, the ancient Celtic priesthood teachers and law givers; the Odinists who follow a Norse or Northern form of heathenism, focusing around the use of Runes as a magical alphabet and the mythology of Scandinavia; there are various kinds of Shamans, some deriving from the original folk healers in the Russian steppes, and some emerging from California or other western sources. A little research will indicate flavours of pagan spirituality, ritual and practice to suit almost anyone.

However, behind and underneath these innovations are the old village witches, going about their business in time-honoured fashion, curing animals and people sick of body or heart, using herbs and plants, making charms with holy stones, and singing spells under the moon. They have read the books, I am sure, but haven't rushed out to call themselves wiccans, or pagans, or anything else. They don't even call themselves witches – that is a word used by those who seek their help – but they draw on a vast and ancient heritage of country wisdom, wit and common sense, which you don't necessarily gain from an initiation. Their myriad arts and crafts are closely linked to the places they live in, their plant knowledge drawn from nearby woods and fields, mountains or rivers within quite a small compass. Their rituals celebrate the produce of their lands, the fertility of their animals or family or minds, and no one recognizes the powers they wield for the benefit of their own community.

Two

MOON MYSTERIES

I am the moon that rises from the sea, the twilight sea,

I bring men dreams that rule their destiny,

bring the dream tides to the souls of men,

the tides that ebb and flow and ebb again ...

These are the moon tides, these belong to me,

Hera in heaven, in Earth, Persephone,

Levannah of the tides, and Hecate,

Diana of the Moon, Star of the Sea.

These are my secrets, these belong to me ...

Dion Fortune, *The Sea Priestess*

The Moon has fascinated people from the earliest times. Through her power the tides of the sea are drawn up, and the tides in our own psychic abilities are able to increase and flow away. By learning about this essential force in our world we can control it in ourselves, to awaken our hidden abilities, to see into the future, to understand our inner selves and to communicate with our creative spirits. Witches use tides and lunar cycles to draw on the useful energies of the Moon, marking passing time by moons. They watch their dreams, and develop the safe art of voyaging in vision, which came from story-telling and the arts of the bards. Most of us recognize that our energy levels fluctuate each month, even during each week, and some of the changes may be led by the moon's pull. It is possible to use this influence to aid everything we do, by aligning our own lives to that of the solar system.

Witches have traditionally been linked with the Moon, for their magic is thought to have always been performed in darkness. It was thought that they would gather at full moons to dance on the heath and call up elemental spirits. Some of the classical Moon goddesses are also associated with prophecy, incantations and strange happenings. One of these is Hecate (pronounced Heh-cat-y) the Roman goddess of crossroads, a location where witches used to meet, and her symbols include a dog, often linked to the underworld, a mirror for divining the future, and a torch to guide her on dark nights. Her name may be related to the older Egyptian god of magic, Heka, for occult working, singing spells, making talismans and performing conjurations have always been aspects of human life.

More recent connections between witches and the Moon are to be found in *Aradia*, by Charles Leland, for his Italian witch, Maddelena, said that Diana, the goddess of hunting, with her silver bow, was one of the goddesses called upon for help with magic:

> ... Adore the spirit of your Queen, the great Diana. She who would
>
> wish to learn the arts of sorcery, yet who has not won its deepest
>
> secrets, Diana will teach her, in truth all things as yet unknown.

One of the oldest known 'goddess' figures is a stone carving from Laussel in the Dordogne in southern France, which is thought to be 40,000 years old. It shows a voluptuous female figure holding up a curved horn-shaped object on which are many cut marks. It is surmised that this represents the moon and the cuts indicate the days between full moons. This seems to show that our very earliest ancestors were interested in the lights in the sky and perhaps demonstrates that a simple record was kept to mark the moon's phases. In the unpolluted skies of the past the moon shone very brightly, and her waxing and waning phases would have been of interest to any watchers below. From the tiniest crescent to the full round brightness and back to nothing would have offered a useful way of marking short lengths of time, clearly observable in a way that the Sun's light does not show.

Many Northern peoples, however, recorded the Moon as a God, which is still remembered in the nursery rhyme, 'The Man in the Moon, came down too soon ...'. The ancient Egyptians associated the moon with their god of wisdom, Thoth, who is depicted with the head of an Ibis: its curved beak is like the shape of the moon and its black and white plumage seems to show the dark and light phases. Thoth was also the god of writing and recording information, perhaps watching the passing of the moon's phases, the annual rising of the River Nile, and other related matters. Some other ancient cultures had moon goddesses and some had moon gods, and if you choose to call upon any of these deities it is always safer and best to stick to gods and goddesses from one tradition, like the Egyptian, Sumerian, Greek or Celtic. Try to find out exactly who you are dealing with before you begin.

Although some people consider darkness sinister and gloomy, there are lots of advantages in working certain kinds of today's magic at night. One is simply that it is quieter. Roads have less traffic, there is less disturbance from neighbours and music, and the world seems to be holding its breath before starting a new day. If you want to take up the arts of witchcraft you will have to find ways which allow you to feel safe out of doors when it is dark. Maybe just going into your own garden and noticing what your neighbours are doing in the evening could be a start. You will need to start to observe the sky, and though it is hard to see many stars against street lights, the moon in most of her phases will be visible, and the planets, especially Venus, the brightest thing in the night sky after the Moon, and Jupiter and Saturn can all be seen with the naked eye, if you can find out where to look. Soon you may discover the brilliant blue-green point of Sirius, the Dog Star which follows the constellation of Orion.

Get hold of a simple star and planet guide for your area if these ideas are new to you and begin to watch the movements of these heavenly bodies. You will find newspapers often give a list of what is visible at what time of night and in which direction, and that is a great help. There are television programmes which regularly show planetary movements and man-made space stations and so on as they cross the heavens. An ordinary pair of binoculars will help you pick out planets and stars and any other nocturnal objects of interest. Never use these to look towards the Sun, even at an eclipse, as you could blind yourself. You will also need to be able to read a compass, in any case, in order to set out magical circles in the most effective way for the festival or ritual.

A very basic exercise is to look out of each of the windows of your home at dawn and dusk to see where the Sun rises and sets, noting which building or section of the horizon it crosses. Look again a week later and discover the changes, and then begin to look at where the Moon is first seen, and where she sets. You will soon discover her pattern is quite different to the Sun's steady progress, and you will have to note with care her movements even against a very built-up and man-made horizon. Draw yourself some diagrams to show why the Moon waxes and wanes, and be sure you can tell which crescent is which at a glance – this is a key to witch magic.

In many modern books there are references to the idea of Triple Moon Goddesses from different cultures but a closer look at the way ancient people dealt with their deities shows this is not the case. As mentioned before, the Egyptians had a Moon God, Thoth, the Romans had Diana the Huntress, or Selene or sometimes Luna, the Greeks named Artemis Lady of the Silver Bow, and Hecate was Goddess of the three ways, Tri-via, meeting at a crossroads. Because other ancient cultures endured for thousands of years, and in that time had different pantheons or collections of gods and goddesses who changed over time, it is hard to find this triple pattern. In any case, once you start to observe the phases of the moon, you will discover there are really four.

The new moon is invisible, because she is too close to the sun to be seen, then there is the first quarter or waxing phase, leading to the full moon, the clearest and most obvious. After the full moon her light wanes until she is dark, before the next new moon. Each of the phases merges into the next, but you can divide each lunar cycle or month into four seven-night parts. Each is associated with different kinds of magic. When the moon is new it is a good time to begin any new project, sow the seeds of plants which will grow into flowers or vegetables which grow above ground, like peas, beans and tomatoes. When the moon is waxing towards full her light, which works on our minds and dreams, will draw things into the open, so it can be the right phase for divination with Tarot cards or other illuminating, picture-symbol systems.

At the full moon there is light enough to go out of doors, explore the secret world of the realm of dreams, hold meetings and aim to have things come to fruition. During the waning to dark phase it was traditional to plant potatoes, carrots or other vegetables where the roots were the important part.

The moon is closely linked with our dreams, and most people, even if they are not aware of it, dream in cycles linked to the moon. At a certain phase which does vary from person to person, your dreams will be brighter, more vivid and easier to recall, and at the opposite time, they will be less colourful and harder to remember. Learning to hold onto your dreams is a very important aspect of witch wisdom, because many dreams actually foretell events from the future, or reveal the activities of our previous lives, teach us how to find healing or offer answers to problems of everyday life. Even if you don't remember them, you will dream, not once, but three or four times in every night of sleep. By making friends with the power of the Moon, using her symbols and acknowledging her phases you will start, gradually, to be able to grasp these fleeting memories and learn their value. It is a skill that every witch should master.

Not only does the moon rule over dreams but all the other dream-like mental states which are essential to effective magic and ritual. These altered states of awareness include western meditation, which differs from eastern meditation in that it produces practical results called 'realizations', when new ideas flash into your mind or mental links between concepts you were familiar with are forged suddenly. The eastern version is more concerned with detachment from the world of maya or illusion, and emptying the mind to stillness. Most western people find this very hard. Meditation is a state of poised mental stillness, when the perceptions are alert while the body is relaxed and at peace. By sitting upright, with closed eyes, and allowing the theme of a meditation, a word or phrase, to drift into your inner perception, these realizations may start to form. Although it is simple, it is not an easy process for most stressed and complex people, and you can't get someone else to do it for you. Such work, like eating food, nourishes the soul. It is an essential skill for all witches, who wish to see the future.

The reverse of meditation is creative visualization, for this is the key to magic. It is a mental art where a clear picture of a place or journey, or a desired result is clearly seen, in the mind's eye, and held there until it becomes reality. Like meditation it is a technique which has to be patiently learned for it really is essential to giving meaning to any act of witchcraft. If you can't see them, how can you meet the gods or goddesses you may wish to work with? If you can't hold an idea in your mind you won't be able to get the real thing to come to you, whether it is a new home or a healed bone or a call from a long-lost friend, or a garden made out of a piece of waste ground.

The witches of old did not sit down and deliberately perform meditations or visual journeys because they would have to do many repetitive tasks in their everyday work. Most old skills require expertise combined with persistence to complete, whether it was hoeing a row of leeks, knitting a jumper, milking a cow or following a herd of sheep at pasture. Many old tasks required very little conscious attention, but involved repeated physical actions which became automatic, in the way that most of us can drive a car and listen to the radio at the same time. Now we have to drive, hear the music, answer the phone and navigate through a strange road system! No wonder modern people are so stressed, and stress is counterproductive to magic. If you want to be a witch you will have to conquer stress and reclaim some time for relaxation, study and practice in your life. Without these, the essential powers of the moon, who can awaken even the most deeply sleeping psyche, will have no beneficial effects.

What helps to turn a modern person into a witch, or perhaps more correctly, awakens the witch powers that everyone potentially has, is not necessarily initiation into a coven, though that can work for some people, but more often it is a simple reassessment of the would-be witch's life. By starting to learn about the moon in the sky, not by consulting watches with moon phase dials or on the internet, you will start to make a connection with that most occult quality of curiosity. By observing your own life, your sleeping and waking patterns, your dreams or lack of them, you will begin to take control of the hidden parts of your life that have been stolen from you by the pressures of mundane existence. Start to notice how you are actually feeling, in body, mind and spirit, every day when you wake. Set aside a few minutes several times during the day to reassess your feelings, and begin keeping possibly the first secret of your magical career. This is a Moon Diary.

A Moon Diary may be any book, of any size, but lots of witches like to choose ones with hard covers in their favourite colour, and sometimes decorate these too. In this book, which needs to be kept entirely to yourself, you should write memories of dreams, any moon observations, any magical work you do, results of meditations of inner journeys. Later on, if you begin to mark out magical circles, perform rituals or learn the arts of divination, this information can be added. Keeping this Moon Book to yourself alone will allow you to be entirely honest, about your own feelings, hopes, desires and wishes. If anyone else were ever to see it, it would prevent this openness, which is an essential step in taking magical control of your life. As you begin to see the shape of the moon changing in the sky, and begin to perceive the changes in your own moods and dreams each month, the records will help to demonstrate to you that these are real experiences. At first it may be hard, fitting in a brief writing session each day, as well as a few minutes' meditation and a little work on your aims, but it really is worth it.

To turn an ordinary life towards that of a witch requires many things. Start with an absolutely honest and in-depth examination of your needs, intentions and motives in all the areas of your life. Consider your body, your family, your job, your relationships with others whether they are friends, relatives or work colleagues. Look at your assets, both financial and time commitments, examine your hobbies and pastimes, and the way you are responsible for things in the different fields of life. Write all of this in your Moon Book, a bit at a time, if necessary, so that you have a record which you can add to and refer back to as you go along. Think hard about how people around you, your parents or work mates, would react if you tell them you are a witch. What will they say? Would they be shocked, or tease or bully you, mock your interest or demand 'spells' to sort out their lives, or would they expect you to turn enemies into toads, or tell fortunes? These are other reasons why your book should be a closely guarded secret, because people who are ignorant as to the ways of witches in the twenty-first century, can be cruel and afraid.

Perhaps you feel ready to begin training yourself in the arts of witchcraft, and want to get started. There are three things which all witches need: Patience, Persistence and Practice. It is no good starting off in a rush; learning magic is like learning another language, for it is the tongue of the inner mind. Like playing a musical instrument, it isn't much good trying something, finding it harder than you thought and then giving up. Only regular effort, which may offer few results to begin with, will give you the awareness and control that today's magic arts demand.

The first step is to try the Moon Breath. You will need to find at least 15 minutes when you won't be disturbed, and can sit in an upright chair. Sit with your spine straight, your feet flat on the floor, and your hands lying loosely in your lap. Close your eyes and begin to sense what you can feel, hear or smell. Allow yourself to relax as much as possible, and think of the Moon. Breathe in slowly through your nose for a count of four, hold your breath in for four, breathe out through your mouth for four, and finally hold your breath out for a count of four. Repeat this ten times, without being distracted. It sounds easy, doesn't it? – well, try it!

Imagine starting at the dark of the moon, seeing the light grow as you breathe in and hold as the full moon. Breathing out see the moon fading to dark again, when you hold your breath out. This is quite difficult and needs many attempts before it comes naturally, and you may have to work out a speed of counting, slow or fast to suit your abilities. Aim to be as slow as is possible, taking into account your state of health, any things which may make it harder to breathe, like smoking (give that up, as an act of magic and self-control!). Continue to relax all your muscles, allowing any tensions to be breathed out and calmness and stillness to be breathed in with every cycle. Try just ten breaths with absolute concentration, and when you have managed that, congratulate yourself.

See if you can do this cycle two or three times every day. It will help you to feel in control of your life, relax tensions at work and, if used when you need to concentrate, it will really help. It is also a first stage towards mastering the magical skills of mind control. This may take quite a few regular and concentrated sessions, but it is worth it.

When you have got this process to work successfully, then you can go on to the next stage. This is to take a word, for example 'Moon', and hold that in your mind after you have done the breathing exercise. Allow ideas, thoughts and concepts to flow through your mental point of attention or inner eye. This is not an exercise in recalling images, but of achieving 'realizations', new ideas which flash into being from old ones. It may help to say a silent running commentary as these thoughts well up from your dreaming mind, so that you can remember them. When you have spent about five to ten minutes at this task, gently come back to ordinary awareness, take three really slow deep breaths and stretch. Immediately write down in your Moon Diary any ideas that have arisen. Be patient with yourself, this simple skill is not easy to master, so try brief sessions, regularly, until it works. It is the links with your inner or dreaming mind which give power to witchcraft and magic.

When you have got results from just one word, try two words, like 'moon tides'. Again you are seeking inspiration in words and feelings, insights and illuminations, not images. Here are a few more basic themes which you can work on, one at a time, for at least five sessions each.

a) 'The moon is the ruler of dreams'
b) 'Blue moon'
c) 'Fair goddess of the rainbow, of the stars and of the moon'
d) 'The triumph of the moon'
e) After you have got realizations from these previous themes, choose three more lunar concepts from books, poetry, or a source of your own choice, for later on you will need to be able to select meditation subjects to increase and strengthen this conscious dreaming awareness.

Although these may all seem simple, some of the ideas actually have a whole collection of magical interpretations, and it is those you are looking for. Try to meditate for just a few minutes every day, because gradually you will establish a clearer connection with the deeper levels of your mind, which will show up as calmness in the day times, and brighter, more memorable dreams at night. This skill will help your powers of divination, give you insights about problem solving and calm everyday situations.

Another kind of basic moon mind magic is the use of creative visualization or inner journeying. With meditation you are making your dreaming mind into an empty cup which will be filled with realizations. In the art of visualization you will draw on memory, imagery and inner creativity to 'see' with your inner eyes, and later with your ordinary sight, pictures and scenes which lie at the heart of practical witch magic.

Again you will need to perform the moon breathing exercise, allowing your body to relax, and become both physically and mentally still. When you achieve this you will know by the floating feeling you have, and how the noises and distractions around you all fade away. Once in this state of relaxed awareness, when your mind is alert and your body absolutely relaxed, begin to think of somewhere you really like. It is best to choose an outdoor scene, and build up not just the picture, but the atmosphere, how you are feeling about it, and the sounds, scents and temperature of that place. Work on this for a couple of weeks, allowing the images to move and develop, just as if you were in that place, interacting with it, as you have done in the past. Concentrate on the setting rather than any people, as these can be distracting at this stage of your magical awakening. Always note down your experiences in your Moon Diary, so that you can see, as months pass, how you are progressing.

The next exercise is to start to imagine or recall a scene which feels safe, at night. Perhaps you can simply remember looking up at a clear night sky, seeing the stars and the moon above you, watching for shooting stars, and noticing how the stars twinkle but the planets shine with a steady and often coloured light. Allow yourself to be really absorbed in this scene, rising mentally, until though feeling secure and still attached to your body, you too can be up there in the heavens, seeing the blazes of heavenly bodies quite close. Try this for five sessions, noting how you feel, what you sense and how much clearer the visions become as you keep at it.

Inner journeying used to be one of the most closely guarded magical secrets, until in the early 1980s an English magical teacher, Gareth Knight, began to run weekend courses at Hawkwood College, where this art, then described as 'Path Working', was taught. This was gradually revealed to students outside the closed doors of qabalistic lodges where it had been used for generations. It was kept secret because, like most arts of magic, it seems simple and harmless, yet it is the essential key to turning dabbling and play acting into efficient ritual and direct connection with the inner forces of gods and goddesses and elemental beings, who are the friends and companions of witches. It has to be learnt, step by step, until you can clearly see images, sense feelings, and experience a reality other than what is around you. There is no way other than regular and concentrated practice to develop the vital skills in this magic of the mind.

Once you have begun to really 'see' with your inner sight you can begin some more basic experiments. These involve making a mental journey to a place where you can gain insights, meet with mythical beings or experience growth in your inner life. Basically it is a way of commanding yourself to dream when you are awake, so that you can interact with beings in that state, learn from them, share their stories and receive all kinds of help.

Find a time and place when you won't be disturbed, shut off all distractions including music, dim the lights and, if you wish, you may light a candle and scent the room with incense or other fragrances. Relax and perform the moon breath until you are poised and ready, close your eyes, then imagine in front of you a great dark screen, filling your entire field of vision. Just allow that plain area to develop in front of your inner eyes. Follow these images, letting each become solid and real before going on to the next. (Pause and take as long as you like between sentences at each set of dots.)

From the darkness, begin to see a country landscape forming ... See around you open fields of grass and wild flowers with a winding path running though them ... Be aware that the temperature is pleasant and that a light breeze is blowing ... It is evening and the sun is setting behind you, turning the sky crimson and gold ... It is very peaceful, and you feel safe and calm ...

Gradually it gets darker and stars begin to appear in the indigo sky ... You continue walking along the smooth path which is now rising up a small hill ... The path gets steeper but is still smooth and you look down at your feet ... Now you are scrambling up a rocky trail where the path shows paler against dark rock ... Suddenly you find that you have climbed over the lip of the rise to stand on a plateau ... Looking around you see darkness with occasional points of yellow light below, and millions of stars above ... A quarter moon is rising in front of you, and for a few moments you bask in her silvery light ...

Sense the stillness and quiet of this rocky knoll, and the brilliance of the stars ... Notice how many different colours they show, as if they were jewels spread on a black velvet cloth ... After a while you look down and see there is a smooth black rock where you can sit looking at the moon ... After a while you look down, and notice that in the top of the rock is a natural circular basin which has filled with rain ... You gaze at the still water and begin to notice it changing, becoming misty and silvery ...

You see that the right hand side of the round pool is shining with a different light, and you are fascinated ... Gradually the light spreads across the whole pool, and continues in a misty way ... You may begin to see shapes moving in the silver light ... Gradually the whole round dip of water is like a mirror and you lean closer ... You may even see your own face, or a vaguer image which will have meaning for you ...

Gently the light starts to withdraw, moving across the face of the water until it is just a silvery rim on the left of the pool ... Your thoughts refocus on yourself and the night sky ... The stars are still bright but the moon is now setting low on the horizon ...

You stand up and stretch, in your vision, seeing the path down the hill is shining with a pale light ... You give thanks to the power of moonlight which may have granted you a vision and begin to follow the path back down the hill ... Take your time, for though going down seems easier than coming up, you need to get back to the open fields slowly and carefully ... Soon you see grass and flowering plants on either side of the path, and the light is growing towards a new day ... You close your inner eyes and breathe deeply, smelling the sweet scents of the flowers, and feeling light on your skin ... When you look again you are back in your own familiar place.

Slowly stretch and breathe deeply, feeling your feet on the floor, the chair beneath you and the everyday things around you. It is a good idea to have

a warm drink and something to eat to ensure you are grounded into your usual reality, and as you do this, note down your experience in the Moon Diary. You can record the narrative of the Inner Journey to use on your own, or with a group, if you prefer. This is an exercise you can share with friends, perhaps one of them reading the details of the journey, pausing after each sentence to allow you all to build up the images. You may need a few moments at the top of the hill to really connect with the visions in the pool, and then a little time at the end to get ready to face the world again. Take things slowly, perhaps going part way to the moon mountain, and then following the path back. It is important to come back the same way until you are really experienced at this art, so that you don't feel disorientated.

Like many of the other arts of witchcraft this is apparently a very simple idea, familiar to all who have had stories read to them and 'imagined' the action, characters and scenery. It is because this is such an old process, for there must have been storytellers among the first people who could speak or sing, and nearly everyone enjoys hearing tales, whatever their age. Used with a trained and focused mind, it is one of the most potent aspects of magic, yet it needs to be learned, and its power understood before it can be applied to the old Craft. Training the mind through concentration is a witch art that you will have to learn for yourself. No coven can reveal it to you, no initiation awaken it, no High Priestess or Priest can make your innate psychic senses become detectable, unless you work on them yourself. Practise the earlier exercises with patience and persistence and you will soon learn if you have what it takes to be a witch.

By getting used to creating and then entering into these inner scenes you are training your awareness to be able to receive the images, thoughts and feelings which are an essential part of many divination or fortune telling arts. By being able to travel in your mind you will find it possible to visit places you love when you can't travel in your body. You will be able to explore the settings of books, whether fact or fiction, travel to outer space, or venture into caves and the otherworld of magical reality. Through these inner journeys you can open doors to the past and the future, seeing scenes just as they happened hundreds of years ago or will happen in the ages to come. Although this appears to be a rather simple and possibly unexciting skill it is very important to learn if you want to open the doors of mental magic. Witches in the past were usually able to do this kind of thing without training because they used the part of their mind which is linked to the imagination much more than we book-bound and literate people do.

Through inner journeys you will be able to meet with the gods and goddesses of your land, share rituals with your ancestors, discover aspects of your past lives, and open up an entire and vast world of the deep mind, which is normally only revealed to us in dreams and visions. Through these gates of dreams it is possible to develop skills at divination with the Tarot cards or other systems, like scrying or crystal gazing, and creativity in everyday life drawing from a deep well of insight and traditional wisdom. It just takes a bit of regular effort, each day, to rehearse these skills and create the inner links between your dreaming mind and your controlling consciousness.

One area of witch magic which you might like to explore is that of using the light of the Moon as actual power. There are many rituals in books by modern witches which purport to 'Draw down the Moon', using knives and cups. This is a very different sort of working than that which actually does draw down moonlight for magical use. You can tell many of the modern witch rites were written by a man, as they have not grown organically in the way that feminine thinking tends to lead them. The male-inspired rites tend to be pseudo-sexual, repressive (binding and flagellation were never parts of the Women's Mysteries), or very rigid.

Men were more often involved with solar rather than lunar rites, for example in Morris Dancing, which is a genuine survival of some very ancient Men's Mysteries. This allows them to dress up, make suggestive gestures with rods and sometimes swords, and prance about in the yard of their favourite pub on a sunny afternoon. That is the proper place for the solar fertility magic, but the moon rites which used to exist were much more gentle, secret and sacred. The symbols of the Moon are nearly all round – bowls, sieves, spindle whorls, mirrors and baskets. These have vanished from ordinary sight, but to those who work directly with the Moon can enter her changed modes of consciousness and re-learn the older rites.

An ancient ceremony, perhaps originally performed by a Grandmother, Mother and Daughter, involved taking a piece of mirror, a bowl and some spring water or wine to a place near still water. At the right phase of the moon for the magic required (for example, to increase health or crops use a waxing moon, and to reduce fever or pain, use a waning phase), the Mother would hold the bowl (probably of pewter, but these days silver or glass), the girl would pour in the water, and the grandmother would watch the light of the Moon in the still pool. Then, carefully positioning the mirror, she would reflect the Moon into the bowl, thus reversing the phase. It is possible to scry in such a mirrored moon-pool, or to seek healing when the Moon's real light is drawn down into the water, or to gain lunar powers by drinking the water or wine, or bathing in it. This can be a very potent ritual, devoid of wordy prayers, not involving any rough gestures or dramatic actions, and it is very different to the fossilized rites in books, for it is vital that all the ladies involved speak, dance, gesture or act spontaneously. You can't write down these old arts, they have to be experienced, felt, and when the inspiration comes it has to be acted on wholeheartedly and immediately.

The Moon provides a marker to the passing nights, and by beginning to align yourself to this aspect of Nature you will start to discover your own insights and intuition. Your awareness begins to increase, especially if you fit in some meditation work. You may be surprised how your dreams do start to become clearer and are easier to recall each morning, and that you get flashes of inspiration which help you solve problems. These are all signs that your own inherent witch powers are waking up, by the light of the moon. Of course, the more time and effort you are able to devote to practice, reading and exploring the world around you the faster and greater your abilities will come. You can help this by the old use of simple workings based on the power of the Moon.

If you want to learn how you can benefit from lunar energies, you could start designing some simple spells. Properly a spell is a collection of words with a clear purpose, often when written appearing as a short poem with effective rhymes and rhythms. These would have been chanted, intoned or sung, or these days because few of us have the courage to sing out loud, spoken clearly and firmly, usually three or more times. A spell must express a single, real and positive intent, and the best ones are written by the would-be spell weaver and should rhyme, if possible. A spell is really a one-off song, which is designed for a particular desire, is chanted with appropriate actions, perhaps within a magical circle on occasion. It is then forgotten or set aside until it has worked.

Traditionally, different phases of the moon are used for different kinds of spells. For example, anything which needs to grow, increase or continue for a time is worked in the waxing phase of the moon, for example if you want help to study and pass an exam. Things which need to fade or diminish, like illnesses or problems, would be bespelled in the waning part of the moon cycle.

Ideally, you will need to write or learn a few basic spells which you have written, to help you make a magical space, to bless yourself and those work-ing with you, to connect the symbols you set upon your altar with the powers you are calling on, and so on. These are very special and personal and need to be thought out carefully by you and your friends, rather than copied from someone else. Spells work best for their maker, who can tailor them to the exact needs of the moment, using words and feelings which are very personal. Although there are books of spells available, few of these work for anyone but the author, but may be used as a guide to help you decide what sort of things to say. Here is a very basic example, but it should be altered by you before you use it, and you should select items which have a personal meaning for you.

Although it looks simple, you will have to make preparations, set aside time, collect suitable items for the elements, lay out a square-shaped table with a clean white cloth and locate a white candle and candle holder, matches and the other symbolic objects mentioned here.

SPELLSPELLSPELLSPELLSPELLSPELLSPELLSPELLSPELL

Here is a Spell to Open the Gates of Dream, which you should alter and build upon, to make it your own.

1 Work out why you want to open the gates of dreaming or inner
   vision and write it down in your Moon Diary. During a waxing
   moon, in the evening when you can actually see her light, set out
   all the equipment, take some moon breaths and relax. When

everything is ready, and you have worked out your own words, you can sing the spell.

2 Place a white stone, a scented flower, a small bowl of water and a lighted candle at the four corners of the table, covered with a white cloth. Find a picture of an open door or gate or draw one, which shows a beautiful view, or clouds. (You will have to use a picture which signifies something which is meaningful to you.)

3 Sit still, relax and focus on your purpose, ideally using the Moon Breath exercise. When you are calm and ready, stand up and make opening gestures to each of the four quarters. Sing something like the following:

Open my mind like a growing flower; as my dreams
    I now empower.
Open my eyes in the candle's light, that my dreams may
    be bright.
Open my soul to the water's flow, that on dream journeys
    I may go.
Open my heart to this stone so cold, that my dreams
    I'll safely hold.

4 Circle round the table slowly, three times, singing: 'Open gates that I may roam and then bring inner wisdom home.'

SPELLSPELLSPELLSPELLSPELLSPELLSPELLSPELLSPELL

You will find that your dreams and inner visions get clearer in the nights after you have done this. A slightly altered version may be used when you start to use the witch arts of scrying in a black mirror, which is much easier to use than a bright glass ball, or if you start to master the Tarot or similar picture divination skills.

What is important is to start to recognize the various tidal energies in your life, the influence of day and night, the effect that each phase of the moon has on your dreams, visions and those very subtle witch-like insights which come so suddenly and are so true. You will gradually realize that it isn't always necessary to be part of a group or to follow the tenets of some religion, ancient or modern, set out in a book. Make friends with your inner mind through watching and trying to understand your dreams. Also be aware how you are becoming more sensitive to the feelings and emotions of the people around you – even potted plants will somehow start to communicate their need for water or attention! These awakenings of psychic sensitivity are very gentle and gradual, but they will clearly demonstrate to you that you do have abilities which can be seen as magical if you find time and space to acknowledge these. They are essential to an effective witch's arts and crafts, and well worth the effort of cultivating, even if they are not so dramatic as being involved in complicated rituals and festival circles.

Three

THE SUN'S SYMBOLS

Oh Sun, visible and tangible of whom this Earth is but a frozen spark,

turning about Thee in its annual and diurnal motion; source of light,

source of life, let Thy perpetual radiance hearten us to continual

labour and enjoyment ...

Aleister Crowley, 'The Gnostic Mass', *Magic in Theory and Practice*

As well as using moon cycles witches have always connected to the turning year, seeing Nature reborn in midwinter, growing though spring, flourishing in the summer, offering harvests in autumn and returning to repose in winter. They also use the symbolic power of the signs of the Zodiac, both in personal horoscopes and as a source of magic. Learning the patterns of stars in the sky and the influences they have on the lives of the people is a very old tradition, and anyone can master the essentials of it. Looking at the way you feel about sunshine, about daylight and the seasons will provide lots of ideas to meditate on. Understanding how you feel now about these great influences can allow you to control those feelings. Perhaps you have room in your philosophy for a Moon Goddess and a Sun God, or several of these deities, or perhaps these are concepts you have never even thought about. There are no 'have tos' in witchcraft. Many modern pagans do have a personal concept of a Sun god or goddess, some are based on classical originals, others are more individual, but it really is up to you.

Just as the Moon rules over the subconscious or dreaming mind, the Sun rules the waking mind, which gives shape to the self. The Sun shines on your persona, the mask behind which most people hide during daily living, for it conceals the tender true self as a crab's shell protects the crab's soft body. In studying the arts and crafts of the witches it is necessary to know the difference, for the waking mind is directed by the will. In magic the true will is not a conscious wish or desire, but a deeper power to make things happen. You may have come across the 'witches' motto', 'An it harm none, do as ye will.' The will here is not a general feeling of 'Oh, it would be nice if ...', but a strong inner impulse of right and truth. It is that kind of 'will' that you need to recognize before you start using magic. It is a compulsion to act which needs to be brought out into the solar light of consciousness before you perform a ritual or spell.

To discover your true will you first need to know who you really are. What is your name? Do you like it and feel it fits how you see yourself? Would you like to change it? Have you changed your name through marriage or for some other reason? Did that make any difference to how you saw yourself? Again, only you know the honest answers to these questions, but they need to be considered in the light of day. Knowing who you are and where you aim to go are some of the first questions anyone searching for wisdom from the ancient Mysteries needs to consider. Without self-knowledge you will have no way of judging the needs of others, because you will have no measure to hold up to them.

A lot of a modern witch's work is involved with helping other people, and so it is essential that every witch understands her or his motives, so that you don't get misled or confused. When you come to learn the arts of divination these perceptions can be vital, for it will help you to give a clear explanation indicated by the Tarot cards or other oracle. You will also realize that if you give advice, some people will act on it, and if it is wrong they will blame you and your Craft for their troubles. No one can guarantee that every divination will come 100 per cent true, or that healing will work, but if you apply common sense based on personal awareness, you are more likely to succeed than not. You can always ask yourself the question, 'If I was given this advice or guidance, would I find it useful and acceptable?'

The first step to understanding other people is understanding yourself, and drawing out into the daylight all those hidden or ignored aspects of yourself that can assist with your magical career. Everyone has a myriad of talents which they don't use, some of which include the subtle, psychic sensitivities that come under the jurisdiction of the Moon, and others are the more obvious skills, which the Sun rules. Witchcraft contains many actual crafts, skills at designing, making, and altering things for your own use. If, for example, you want to create a talisman you may have to carve wood, paint colours, sew a protective bag, blend incense, and calculate the correct planetary hour to perform a consecration ritual which you have written. These are just a few of the many techniques which old fashioned witches knew, and there are lots more. Many of these are practical skills that are useful in everyday life. For example, if you learn to bake sacred cake for a festival, you can also enjoy making others for fun. If you wish to wear special garments for your rituals you shouldn't just buy them, but stitch them with your own hands. Yes, in today's world you can buy robes, pre-blended incenses, published books of rituals and all kinds of expensive equipment, but that is shopping, not witchcraft!

Witches create most of the things they need for their spells and incantations because by doing so they put parts of themselves into the work, they form those powerful bonds with the unseen through which the energies of magic can flow to earth, and make the magic work. A bought thing is just a bought thing, it has no heart or soul, and will not assist in witchcraft unaltered. In the past there were no magical emporia or mail order suppliers of incenses; everything a witch used had to be sought, or created or blended, and it was not just the physical collection of dried plants for incense, for example. Knowing which plant connected to which planetary or other influence made it part of the recipe, which could have been handed down for generations, or invented on the spot to meet a new situation. The medieval grimoires make fascinating reading but they don't supply details of talismans to protect your car from break-ins, or your computer from viruses – a modern witch's arsenal may contain processes for both.

As well as looking at who you are it is important to begin to understand what you believe. Many modern books explain that wicca is a pagan religion based on ancient roots. That may be true, but there are no discoverable direct links, nor any traces in the lives of everyday people through the ages, that in Europe there was any kind of organized pagan faith. There are no records of gatherings for worship, nor descriptions of a priesthood from which today's

High Priestesses and High Priests in wicca may derive their authority. These titles and beliefs were really first made public by Gerald Gardner, Doreen Valiente and later Alex Sanders, and then many more writers, commentators and adherents to this new religion in Britain, where it began, and later in America and the rest of the world. From a few small-circulation books, a whole vast and complicated, hierarchical religious impulse has arisen. It came to light from very small beginnings, but grew like a vast tree, to spread out across the world and answer many spiritually-lost people's prayers for guidance.

Today, because orthodox religions are playing a smaller part in what is now generally a secular society, people are freer to look for new spiritual directions. In the early part of the twentieth century, Dr Carl Jung, one of the founders of psychoanalysis and modern psychology, wrote that everyone has a number of basic drives. These include the need to have shelter, to find food, to have a mate to continue their genetic line, and also an innate need to worship. It is this spiritual need which many facets of modern living had repressed, until it burst forth, in the middle of the twentieth century, as all kinds of 'New Age' beliefs and practices. At first there was an interest in Eastern religions with Indian gurus and teachers introducing meditation, mantras and retreats. These were seized upon by the pop stars of the day, and became much more widely known and talked about. Other influences have come and gone, some based on the writings or experiences of particular authors, and others including the Green and ecological movements. Some are very spiritual and austere, others are political and involve loud public demonstrations. These are all aspects of peoples' individual quests for a different point of view, religion or philosophy.

Although joining a coven will imply that you accept a belief in the Goddess as one or many, and in her Son/consort, the old village witches were not specific about their religious observances. Whatever and however you come to worship, is something you will need to decide for yourself. If you are happy with the idea of many deities who, like gods from other nations, or Christian saints, all have specific tasks, and may be invoked to bring particular benefits, that is a matter for your own heart. But it has to be real. Only by assessing your deepest inner desires for knowledge of the Goddesses and the Gods and finding personal and valid ways of turning a vague interest into a solid faith, can you really become a pagan. By mastering the arts of meditation and inner journeying you can open a clear connection between those in the unseen realms and those on Earth. When that link has been forged you will be able to turn a belief into an experience, and it is then that the deities become real for you.

One of the things held against orthodox religions is that they go out seeking converts. Almost everyone will have seen chanting mystics in the street or had missionaries on the doorstep trying to sell them some aspect of a world faith. None of those uninvited visitors will have been a pagan, trying to convert anyone to their spiritual path. If you do decide to become a pagan that impulse has to come from within. However, the magics used by old witches in the countryside did not depend on any kind of religion. They were applications of what Granny Weatherwax in the Discworld novels of Terry Pratchett calls 'headology'. If you can train your mind to see into the future, connect with healing energies, feel sympathy with others and master the dozens of practical skills of witchcraft, then you can become a witch, should you choose to do so.

Witchcraft is about observation. It is knowing what your neighbours are doing and why, it is knowing the causes of illness and unhappiness and discovering cures, it is about watching the phases of the Moon and the movements of the Sun through the seasons which indicate the subtle magical currents for good or difficulty which flow through the world. Witch magic is about navigating the unseen currents of energy, in the same way a round-the-world yachting crew will sail with the wind and tide, making the best use of natural forces, in order to reach their goal. By observing the patterns of clouds and waves the most ancient sailors were able to find their way across oceans and into safe landfalls. By watching seabirds migrate into the west then return in the following spring they could understand that there were other lands hidden by the curve of the ocean's horizon. By watching the birds which lived under their own eaves departing in the autumn and returning in the spring they could detect shifts in weather patterns. We now have satellites to watch the clouds and scientists to predict the weather, but we still get wet in the rain, and blown about by the winds, if we aren't careful.

Observation and curiosity are essential to any witch, for by seeing what is happening now, in the lives of friends and family, it is possible to predict what might happen next. By seeing, with clear and true sight, the real events of the world around you, you can start to foretell things to come. These insights only come from actual observation, and though it is now possible to enter a virtual world, attend virtual rituals and discover virtually anything you want through modern technology, it has nothing of the power of witchcraft. Old magic can see through time and space, and in our heads we all have far more computing power than the most powerful machine. This comes free at our birth and can be expanded with use. By learning to awaken the sleeping potential of our dreaming minds we can smell the flowers in some distant scene, we can fully participate in a ritual, we can discover the future.

Another basic part of witchcraft is concerned with the energies of the land and its seasons. By watching the plants growing in spring, by watching the trees sprouting leaves, flowers, fruits and then changing to their autumnal colours and shedding their foliage to a barren winter, before the next spring arrives, you will begin to understand such theories as reincarnation. Human souls are born, grow, mature, flourish, perhaps have children, decline and die, but they are immortal, and after rest and reassessment of their soul's journeys, they will return to life in a new body. Earth has her seasons, and it is by aligning to the great forces of Nature which, just like the powers of the tides, have immense force, a witch can work her will.

You may be fortunate to live in a place were you have a garden, or are near a park or farmland, because then you can begin to notice all the small things. What plants are growing now? What flowers are in bloom, or have just set seed, or are yet in bud? Is it winter and the land seems barren and dead? You know that land will become fruitful again, as the seasons pass, but what are the heralds of those changes? Start to be aware of the feel of the sun or wind on your face, the taste of rain, the smell of autumn, when the first frosts start to silver the grass, and there is a lingering scent of woodsmoke in the air. Become light and open to the very gentle shifts of temperature, wind direction, heat or cold of the breeze. This way you will start to awaken your ancestral powers of knowing, that most witchy sixth sense.

Start to look around you at the buildings and shape of the land. When were things built, what was there before? If you can work in a garden, see what the soil is like. Is it heavy clay, sand, good loam or less fertile rocky earth? What grows well in your neighbourhood, and what won't grow at all? Where do the things you eat come from before they reach the shelves in the supermarket? Can you buy organic and local produce in a farmers' market? Here you will start to see the actual effects of the Earth Mother, the Goddess of Nature, if you like, on the things around you. Her effects are gentle, seemingly slow, but they are continuous, and it is by connecting into that vast force that witches draw on the power of the land. It is the energy or life and creation, and can be used to heal, to help your spirit grow, and to reveal the future.

Watch the Sun as it rises and sets. Does it always rise and fall in the same places? How far does it shift from its resting place at the Winter Solstice, to the Summer Solstice, when again it stands still? Perhaps you can take pictures of the most spectacular sunsets, or try to determine just when and where the sun will set on the Equinoxes in Spring and Autumn. Really start to observe, seeing with both your inner and outer vision, what is going on about you, especially any of the signs of Nature. It may be easy to look things up rather than go and witness them for yourself, but you are limiting your vision to a two-dimensional picture. You need to learn to use all of your six magical senses, those of the body and the sixth sense of insight or psychic knowing.

If you are inclined to seek out a personal spiritual path based on the new paganism, you will need to decide which energies and powers are important to you. There are plenty to choose from. Essentially there is the Earth, both as a planet and as the ground beneath your feet, which has been called Gaia, or the Earth Mother or Mother Nature. She provides our home, our food, our clothes, and everything we have is directly or indirectly produced from the structure of the Earth. Beneath the surface, both physically and metaphorically, there is the Underworld. In psychological terms, this can be seen as the subconscious mind, for it contains a store of memories, ancestors and tradition, and is the original home of many myths and legends. Because it is approached through dreams and visions it is often seen as the realm of the dreaming mind. It is not explored by caving expeditions but through meditation and inner journeying.

The Earth may be our home planet and supplier of all our material needs, but it is only one part of a dynamic cycle of life, our Solar system, circling our home star, the Sun. The stuff we are made of is essentially star stuff for we all derive from the same basic materials of the whole of creation. We may now be able to understand the solar system with its central star and an ever-increasing number of planets, moons, asteroids and comets, but we are still dependent on light and energy from the Sun to survive. It is for this reason that most ancient civilizations named a god or sometimes goddess of the Sun. The interaction between the Sun and the Earth gives us our seasons, each special in its own way, offering new harvests of foods or new insights about eternal truths.

Witches knew that both the Sun and Moon affect the growth of plants, that the moon's phases rule the tides of the sea, and that the changing seasons give patterns to the life and work of country people. In Britain before 1700, about 80 per cent of the population was involved in the work of the countryside, on farms and in villages. Even those who worked at trades did so in the original cottage industries of weaving cloth, spinning wool, making cheese, shoes or candles. Within 150 years, about 70 per cent of the population had shifted to towns, cities, industry, factories and foundries. There were fewer farm workers and country crafts, fishermen and agricultural labourers. It was this shift which finally severed the links with Nature for a large chunk of the population.

In ancient cultures the Sun god has many names, including Ra in ancient Egypt, Helios and Apollo in the classical world, Lugh, Bel or Bran in Celtic tales and thousands of other names and titles in other parts of the world. Any good book on mythology will reveal to you the stories of the Sun gods and their adventures in respect of human beings. Many of the names of both gods and goddesses have an actual meaning which tells us something about their speciality or powers. Many of the names of sun gods, not surprisingly, translate as the Bright One, the Shining God, Light or Fire. The sun's light is essential to our own lives, for without the light and the heat from the sun this planet would become a dead ball of rock. There is something sensual about the first warm days of spring when the sun's rays can touch your skin and warm it after a long, wet and dim winter, and seeing the first flowers start to push up through the barren earth can be inspiring.

Although goddesses are often associated with the Earth, the Underworld, the Moon and the seas, the gods are frequently linked to the sky, the winds, the Sun and wild animals. In some old pictures the male deity is shown with either solar rays or horns or antlers. All are symbols of the sun's radiant power. Different versions of how these great deities related not only to Earth, but to the people, make up the underlying mythologies of many pre-Christian religions. Some of these stories have been adopted, reinterpreted and incorporated into the Books of Shadows of modern pagan wiccans. You will have to examine your own relationship with the sun, and whether you feel drawn to worshipping or acknowledging the Lord of Light as a personal deity.

In some traditions the sun is linked to healing, for example, the Greek god Apollo used music played on his seven-stringed lyre to bring health and calm. The sun affects the qualities of herbs and twigs used in healing, and the old witches would have chosen the precise moment when the sunlight had dried the dew from the leaves, but before the flowers opened, to gather many of the medicinal plants. Old writers on the properties of plants attributed each of these to the rulership of the Sun or the other planets, and diseases were also linked to the planets. Cures needed to be found which balanced the heavenly influences upon both the illness and the plant which could cure it. The witches, who used plants for all kinds of magical and medicinal things, would be well aware of the effects of the heavenly bodies on the materials they collected. It is easy to see many of the planets in the night sky if it is not polluted by artificial lights or industrial fumes, so the healers would watch to see when the greatest healing influence would be in the plants they picked.

Once you begin to observe the movements of the sun in the sky, especially at sunset or sunrise, those times of mystical twilight, when the world breathes out, you will start to awaken your own inner point of divine sunlight. This will be shown by an increase in sensitivity to the feelings of others, a greater self-confidence, and assuredness in your daily life. As you continue to meditate, using the symbols associated with the sun, like 'Light', 'Dawning of a new day', 'A Circle' and so on, you will acquire deeper insights. Begin to consider how you might symbolize the power of the sun in your own life and magic. Gold is often seen as a solar colour, and a circle with a dot in the centre is the astrological sign for the sun. In rituals a yellow or gold candle may be used to invite the healing light of the sun to shine upon someone who is not well. Sunlight, if you don't get burned, can be helpful to the body, increasing the supply of vital vitamin D, which wards off diseases, and can be lacking in winter.

Because the most ancient symbol of the sun is a circle, this is used a lot in magical work, to create a place of psychic safety and mental quiet, called a

Sun Sanctuary. To make your own solar circle, begin by placing an upright chair in a clear space. Actually that is all you need, but if you want to make more of a ritual out of the process, to help your mental calmness, you can do so once you have tried the most basic method. This can be done out of doors, too, if you have an undisturbed place where you can sit for a few minutes. Sit still on your seat, and close your eyes. Become aware of any sensations, sounds or other intrusions. If you can cut these off physically, do so, and settle down again.

Next, imagine a clear point of solar fire in your solar plexus, just below your ribs. Feel this as warmth and sense it spinning into a tiny globe of pure and cleansing fire. Each time you breathe in, allow the globe to enlarge, and as you breathe out see it glowing brighter, a golden white colour. Continue, gently enlarging this sphere of solar light until it includes all of you and the chair you are sitting on. Remain still and continue relaxing. Feel the purity of the light flowing through you, driving away any doubts or distracting thoughts.

Keeping your eyes shut, begin to imagine that the great globe of light is protecting you and enclosing your own personal sacred space, which is within the ancient Sanctuary of the Sun. It contains only things of light and peace. Imagine clearly before you a hilly horizon over which the sun is beginning to rise. You are high up, so you see a lot of sky, gradually changing from deep blue to gold, amber, peach and pearl before you. You feel a cool breeze, scented with mountain flowers or pine trees, and you breathe deeply. When this image is clear, and the disc of the sun is just rising say to yourself this silent affirmation: 'I begin!'

Then, mentally looking to your right, see a beautiful summer scene, with flowery meadows, rich farmlands, fruiting orchards and gardens of your favourite blooms. There is birdsong in the trees, and all around you is the scent of roses. Sense that the sun is overhead, but its warmth and light are pleasant but not burning. When this image has developed fully, affirm, 'I shine!'

Using your developing magical senses see behind you, and discover a seascape, edged by a sandy shore. The waves are small, but you hear the rush and swish of them on the sand, and smell the salt breeze, but also the scent of the falling leaves of autumn. Far out on the horizon, the sun is setting, in gold and scarlet, among streaks of fiery cloud, but below that the sea is deep blue green and very calm. When this feeling is strong, say, 'I flow!'

Now look to your left and discover a rocky landscape, seen by starlight upon snow. Sense the utter stillness of midnight, and the depth and strength of the mountains and stones beneath you. Hear owls or night creatures, the witches' companions, calling. Smell woodsmoke and sink into the underlying stillness and silence, allowing your inner perceptions to get stronger. When these images are complete, say to yourself, 'I endure!'

Lastly, return your senses to your own inner heart, that centre point of stillness and balance from which your magical self can emerge. See the tiny but eternal point of soul-light burning in your solar plexus, defending you from any intrusions, linking with the power of magic. Feel it as a gentle warmth, always with you, to guide and inspire you. As you acknowledge this point of eternal inner fire, say, 'I transform!'

Allow your vision to perceive yourself sat in a bubble of golden-white light, encompassed within the landscapes, seen dimly, forming a circle outside the globe. Be aware that this is a magical reality, and a sacred place where you are beyond ordinary time and space. Learn to build up each stage, a step at a time, until your feelings, senses, visions and hearing make these solid around you. Within this still, glowing, golden sphere you will be able to feel protected, not only from dark forces, but also from the everyday disturbances, noises and other distractions which prevent you gaining meaningful realizations, or clear inner visions. It will become a place between realities where you can work all the positive magics, weave all the spells, and discover healing arts in safety and isolation.

When you are certain you have built your sanctuary completely, begin to see the whole thing shrinking around you, gently wrapping you in warmth and safety, until it has diminished to the tiny point of light which it came from. Close your hands over this, give thanks to the light which gives you life, and open your eyes. It may feel a bit strange at first, because you are consciously opening gateways to your dreaming perceptions, so that you can control them. As you become accustomed to the feeling you can, like most witches, use this link to the worlds beyond to see into the future, or at a distance, or to seek healing skills. Get up and stamp firmly on the ground, perhaps have a snack and a drink to complete the process. As you get used to this exercise it will get quicker, deeper and more useful.

When you have completed what ever work you are doing, even if it is only a brief meditation, or the study of a single Tarot card, give thanks. Thank the power of light which brings illumination, strength of purpose and security to perform your magical work. It is as well to complete every session with another statement, 'I complete!'

Although most magical workings take time to come into being, and grow like a seed sown in the earth, the first step has been done, hopefully to your satisfaction. The arts of witchcraft are not things, like life, which you can rehearse. It is always for real, from the first occasion. It is better to prepare well, set out any equipment, symbols, matches for lighting candles and joss sticks and so on before you begin, than getting halfway through an invocation only to discover you overlooked some vital component of the spell.

It does take time, but if you can master the golden solar sanctuary around you, it will help your meditations and inner journeys, and later on the arts of witchcraft. Some people say they can't see, but everyone has memories, everyone has dreams and anyone can *see* if they want to. It is a skill like riding a bicycle, hard at first but easier with practice. Just keep at it until it works. When you understand the principles of this golden globe of sunlight, using similar affirmations you can also create your own Moon Orb, to assist you when scrying or divining with cards, or seeking psychic guidance. The moon can also protect and calm your sacred circle, and later the Sun Sanctuary and the Moon Orb can become the first sacred inner places where you can get to meet the Sun gods for their healing power or the Moon goddess with her silvery powers of insight and wisdom.

When you have managed to really sense the four directions you can meditate on the words, especially the affirmations. Each has many levels of meaning which will become clearer in time. Later you may change these, but only because you have found more meaningful words or phrases, not because you haven't understood the underlying principle. If you want to set up a physical altar, you can look to this exercise for inspiration. Ideally, you will need a round flat space on which you may place symbols which have meaning and spiritual value to you. This is not something you display to visitors to show off your collection of magical equipment, but a private place where you can deepen your connections to the Earth and sky, to Nature and to the powers of creation.

Before you, at the point of sunrise, you could place any small thing which represents beginning, the Element Air or the wind. It could be a bell, or a feather, or something scented with your favourite perfume. Use your inspiration to discover what is right for you, especially if it is natural rather than manufactured. Go round to the summer quarter and find something for warmth, light, sunshine and joy. It could be a flame-coloured flower, a pumice stone from a volcano or a picture of a summer's day in all its glory, as a representative of the Element Fire. The choice is yours.

In the direction of the sea, you can obviously have a dish of sea water, if you are near the ocean, or spring water from a sacred source. You might like to concentrate on colours, or textures, or the scent of autumn leaves. This is a symbol of the Element Water. There are lots of clues to follow up to discover the first symbols which are important to you. The fourth direction is of darkness and winter, but it is also the most important. Without the stability of the ground beneath us we would have no being, so something good and solid is best in this quarter. Perhaps a rock or stone from somewhere you love, but make sure you can freely take it. It is a representation of the supporting strength of the Element Earth.

This is no excuse for knocking pieces off ancient monuments, or buying crystals blasted out of another nation's sacred hills to make trinkets for rich foreigners. If you have collected something from a beach, or dug it out of your garden, or even explored the piles of excavated material by some roadworks to see what kinds of stones come out of the trench, you will be led to discover an appropriate symbol of the Earth. Lastly, in the centre there needs to be light. It could be a small candle, tea light or even a clear glass marble, an image of the Sun or a mirror. See what feels best for you as it stands for the life-giving force of Spirit, or its old name, Aether. You can start out with one set of symbols and as you learn more, these may change. After all, magic is an art of causing changes in accordance with your will, and that is what this is supposed to be.

It will help you to have a basic knowledge of the Signs of the Zodiac, and what the dawning of the Age of Aquarius really means. Ancient people, who observed the sky over many generations, discovered patterns or constellations of stars, forming a great ribbon around the Earth which on a clear night we can still see. As the sun rose each morning and the stars faded it was just possible to see which pattern was there, so it was possible to say 'The Sun is in Pisces or Leo', for example, especially as this continued for about four weeks, giving us the idea of twelve signs of the zodiac. These signs moved in a slow and steady fashion throughout the year, but dancing in front of them, sometimes stopping or even appearing to turn back were the 'travelling stars' or planets as we know them now, as well as the Sun at the centre of the solar system and the Moon, Earth's satellite.

It is the relationship between all these visible lights in the sky that gives rise to the individual horoscope, when their positions are frozen at the moment of birth. Each planet affects the Earth through gravity, and the ancients believed it also influenced everything on the earth through some kind of magical power. Astrologers still believe this, and now some scientists are discovering that a good proportion of successful writers have one configuration of planets, certain sports stars have another, many doctors are governed by a third setting and numerous scientists by a fourth. Michel Gauquelin, who set out to prove astrology was unscientific and inaccurate, was actually surprised to discover the correlations, and had to rethink his assumption. Popular astrology found in newspapers may be of little use, but the principles of each individual being born in a unique and invisible three-dimensional web of planetary and starry influences does make sense. The old witches certainly would have observed such patterns in the dark skies at the births of children they brought into the world, and learned how plants and situations are influenced by heavenly phenomena.

Astrology, like any of the other esoteric arts, can take a lifetime to master fully, but a basic knowledge of the symbols, colours, numbers and incenses for each planet, the time of year and sign of the zodiac which most beneficially influences magical acts is worth learning. You can get this kind of information from books but it ought to be backed up by some personal observations. If you can get out into places where the sky is clear and starry at night and begin to recognize the great patterns of stars which make up the constellations and signs you will be doing what the old witches have done throughout history. You will be able to learn to tell the time by the stars, recognize the ever-turning ribbon of light around the earth and the signs of the zodiac within it. By being able to find the Pole Star you will encounter the axle of heaven, the one fixed point in the night sky of the northern hemisphere, or the Southern Cross which circles the sky of the southern hemisphere. This knowledge is fascinating, and it will bring a witch far closer to the great powers of Nature than being indoors, in an electrically-lit room, making offerings to a plastic image. The Creator made the stars, and that power of re-creation may be drawn into the hands of true witches, to shape and improve the situations around them.

If that isn't possible, you might like to work with solar influences in a different but equally natural way. You may wish to explore the 'Immortal Hour' of the Sun where you need only to get out under the sky. This is a pilgrimage not of distance but of effort. Rise before dawn and stand barefoot in your garden, watching the light of day fill the sky, seeing, if you can, the circle of the sun edge over the rim of the earth. Listen to the stirring of the birds, the unfolding of the petals of the flowers and their day-fresh scents. Spend time in silent communication with the Creator of Day, the bringer of Light, and learn your own way to spread the light of knowledge on your world. It might in time lead you to acknowledging a great solar deity, and name him as did the Greeks, Egyptians or Romans, but that has to be a heartfelt experience and true worship.

You can make the pilgrimage of twilight, or dusk or of the gloaming, wandering in that magical hour that turns light to dark, when the stars come out, and if the moon is new, see her slim crescent setting in the west, behind the sun. Learn how and where the sun and moon set and move along the horizon, how high they stand at their varying zeniths. This is part of the real Craft, of knowing the wild power and using it harmoniously in your own life, to heal, bless, inspire and guide. This can't be learned indoors, from a book, or experienced within a coven circle inside a building, no matter how devout. Being limited by walls blots out not only the light of these heavenly bodies, but their subtle energies, the atmosphere of hushed expectancy as you await moon rise, or the absolute stillness at the dead of night when much of the modern world sleeps. That is the time of magic and witchcraft.

You could, perhaps, make your next whole year, beginning at the Spring Equinox, a solar adventure, setting out goals of places to visit, deities to implore, experiences to gain and new lessons to learn. Make a plan to go to old sites of ancient secrets, standing stone circles and monuments to the cycle of the Sun. Try to enter them with a quiet soul, open to what they may teach. Go to sacred places of other faiths, see what power or not lies there. After all, many churches harbour Green Men, Old Gods of Nature, and many others stand in the shadows of ancient and sacred yews, far older than the new religion. Learn to be open to experiences which don't have fancy names or psychological explanations. Seek out the voices in silence which teach, so that your whole life becomes a Pilgrimage, dedicated to the Great Mother who gave us everything we hold precious. And then, when you have a tale to tell, share it with other travellers on the ancient Sacred Path.

Four

MAGICAL MOMENTS

We lack not rhymes and reasons,

As on this Whirligig of Time,

We circle with the seasons.

Alfred Lord Tennyson, 'Will Waterproof's Lyrical Monologue'

Much of practical witchcraft consists of two different approaches, the immediate and the longer term. The immediate acts of witchcraft are all the traditional things, the spell needed for healing, the Tarot divination which is needed now, or the advice which has to be given right away. These are very much parts of the country witch's repertoire, whereas the longer-term activities are more likely to be associated with coven witches, who plan their festival dates, their working esbats a long time ahead. The abilities to deal with the instant request for help require a witch to have a lot of common sense. Nearly all magic workers, whether witches or ceremonial magicians, prefer to have time to deal with any problems rather than acting immediately. You see, although magic can have instant and amazing results it is usually as a result of years of preparation. To get even a simple spell to do just what you require with no side effects or unexpected results takes a great deal of patient work.

This is due to everything in the Universe being connected. You can't affect one thing without, in some way, affecting the whole galaxy. If there were no connections and every person and situation was separate, then magic wouldn't work, because it would have no way by which power could be transferred from one place to another. To quote Ursula le Guin, 'To light a candle is to cast a shadow!' Think about that. Karma states that every action will cause a reaction. Take a case of healing. Suppose you have an old aunt who is sick and you want to do a healing ritual for her. How would you go about it? Well first of all, you have to be asked by her to intervene. Oh yes, you might think, but I am doing a healing spell, she would want that. She might well want it, but unless she actually asks you to do it you are acting against her will. That is black magic, as is any act which affects a person who has not expressly asked for help, because, unless you are God, you can't know when even your own aunt's lifespan is completed, and perhaps it is her time to die. Perhaps she really needs rest in a caring environment like a hospital, or has to discover that the way she lives is bad for her health. Maybe she could recover quickly from this particular ailment but then need on-going care. Are you ready and willing to provide that, after you have done a quick-fix spell to help her? Do you know the answers to these questions so completely that you know healing is the right answer? Or do you just want to show off your new witchcraft skills and meddle in someone else's karma?

It is particularly true of 'love spells' which cause no end of trouble. Again you might think that making someone fall in love with another person has to be good. Now think how you might feel if you suddenly were made to fall madly in love with someone you weren't attracted to. Wouldn't you feel manipulated? Wouldn't you feel anger that someone else should intervene in your life without your permission? To alter the life path of anyone else is a grey area and should never be attempted. It does happen, and then it is up to more experienced witches to sort out the mess, unweave the spells, but seldom can they repair the harm done to friendships and an individual's sense of self-confidence. There are ways to offer help in both the above situations, but only a lot of work on understanding human needs, predicting all the possible outcomes of any action, and really being willing to deal with the end result can make you a successful witch who really can operate under the adage 'If it harms nothing, do your magic.'

To begin with, it is far safer to learn about the great tides and cycles of the year so that you can gently encourage their powers to flow through your life, developing your skills and sensitivities. That way you will know when you can safely use your wishes and prayers to help in solving someone else's problems. You can always apply that dull old art of meditation to any problem, finding time to be still and create the inner cauldron into which the drops of inspiration may fall from Mother Nature, to guide inspire and direct you to do what is best. Using deep thought you will open yourself to insights and knowledge which go far beyond your own limited problem-solving skills, and so find good and lasting ways of dealing with the requests for help you may receive.

It is written, 'To every thing there is a season, and a time under heaven, a time to sow and a time to reap, a time to dance and a time to weep.' Choosing the right moment to perform an act of magic, celebrate a seasonal festival or call upon the power of the Moon has always been very important. Knowing when something will happen, or when something should happen, was part of the way of the witch, and learning to align your life to Nature's drumbeat can bring all kinds of mental and spiritual rewards. Looking at significant periods in your own life, when things were going well or not so well, and seeing what signs predicted these changes, is a skill to master.

Those who strive to reforge those natural connections to the land and the seasons, to the fields and woods, the oceans and the moorlands, are having a hard task. But it is essential that you start to recognize the passing seasons, because there are great tides of creative energy which can be harnessed for witch magic. It is a very different practice to dancing around a circle in an indoor coven meeting led by a High Priestess, to standing on a high hilltop in the dark, meeting the Lord of the Sky powers, and the Lady of the Earth in their own environment. The natural and wild forces which the old witches used in their spells and incantations were drawn from the very conditions around them, rather than from the intellectual and symbolic powers of the ceremonial magician. Both kinds of magic workers used their own trained insight to sense and direct these forces, but they came at them from different directions.

Out of doors you are already in a sacred circle, the horizon, and every part of the earth, be it virgin forest or city wasteland, partakes of the powers of Nature. In a street you can find soft and squashy mushrooms pushing up through concrete, and wind and weather can destroy the toughest man-made object. Give Nature an inch and she will take over the whole landscape. It has been postulated that if humans vanished from the Earth, in about forty years few traces of our presence would be visible on the surface. The plants and trees from gardens would start to seed and spread into any piles of fallen leaves, unswept by human hands. Grasses, moss and lichens would flourish in the less-polluted conditions, and seeping water would start to undermine buildings and roads, converting them through time into rubble and flattish ribbons of greenery. In the most unlikely conditions, at the bottom of the sea, in the antarctic ice, in hot springs and barren lava fields, life shows itself, in simple forms, but later on in more complicated ones. It is this essential desire by Nature to continue that old witches could draw on for their magics.

Although modern covens, because they meet in groups, need to organize dates well in advance, anyone who links their witchcraft to Mother Nature will have to take their timing from her. Whether you desire to worship the Old Ones, the great powers of the Earth and the Sun and Moon, or named deities from any land or tradition is entirely up to your conscience, but many people appreciate a cycle of feasts and celebrations during the year.

Recent accurate mapping of some of the vast earthworks called 'cursuses' from the Latin for racecourse, and the earliest chambered tombs in Britain and elsewhere, show that many of them are aligned to the midwinter solstice sunrise. One spectacular example of this is the great barrow at Newgrange in Ireland. This huge structure has been reconstructed and refaced with the glistening white quartz rocks which once covered it. But it is not the beauty of its covering, or its setting, but the mathematical precision by which a 'roof box' over the doorway admits the light of the rising sun only around the winter solstice. Then shafts of low light penetrate right to the back of the stone chamber, with its mysterious carved monoliths.

Out of doors the huge cursuses, some over a mile long, are also aligned to face this 'rebirth of the Sun' at the time of its winter standstill. Some of these structures, which are more than 4,000 years old, have burial mounds or other round, bell or disc barrows near to them. It has been suggested that because the Sun is apparently reborn in winter, those whose remains lie nearby may also be reawakened to life at the same time. Many other ancient structures which align to points on the horizon of the midwinter or midsummer sunrise, and occasionally the sunsets, indicate that there must have been a succession of sky watchers who noted these significant points, possibly over hundreds of years. Some horizon positions are marked by standing stones, cairns of small rocks, natural intersections of two hill slopes or notches deliberately cut out of them, all visible some distance away.

Clearly, people were interested in these natural phenomena, and continued to observe and mark significant sunrises over long periods of historical time. Similar features are being discovered in many parts of the world, and now that aerial photographs and satellite mapping can show details of places not much visited on the ground, a deeper understanding of humans and landscape is emerging. Although there is no known connection between the stone age peoples who constructed these sky marks and later inhabitants of the lands, a number of later religions celebrated the same time of year. In Persia a god called Mithras spread in popularity throughout the Roman Empire. His cult, which was a Mystery religion for men only followed the Legions across much of Europe and his priests constructed temples and Mithraiums to his worship in caves and cellars. His special day was 25 December, and he was a Sun god who was born in an animal shelter on that day. In the northern hemisphere, 25 December is the date when it is clear that the days are starting to lengthen from the shortest day of the winter solstice. The Sun/son is returning and the bitter, barren months of winter will start to retreat. Although Yuletide, from the solstice until about 6 January, is celebrated in many northern pre-Christian traditions, it is not one of modern wicca's most important sabbats.

In fact, the Sabbats which many wiccans celebrate are based on the life cycles of animals which some have never seen in their own environment. It seems that sheep played a very important part in the lives of country people. Their wool provided the raw material for cloth, as well as spinning, weaving, dyeing, sewing and selling. Ewes' milk was and is made into cheese and the flesh provided nourishment in warming soups and stews, roasts and cutlets. Their skins were worn with the wool on in winter or could be scraped and preserved to make parchment or leather. Their bones could be carved and those with horns provided the curved tops for shepherds' crooks and walking sticks. There is very little in a sheep that went to waste, for even their shoulder bones were burned in the fire and the resulting patterns of cracks read as an oracle.

In traditional shepherding ewes give birth quite early in the year, producing a first harvest from their flocks in the form of ewes' milk as well as the lambs. One of the festivals celebrated by modern witches is that of Candlemas or Oimelc, Ewe's milk, early in spring. This time is the Feast of St Brigid, and some writers have given her a more pagan ancestry as a Goddess of Crafts, particularly smithying, poetry and healing. She is the patroness of many sacred or healing springs of water under variations of her name as Bride or Brigit. Because the first flowers, snowdrops or 'snow piercers' as they are known in some areas, begin to send up their spiky leaves and white and green flowers, modern pagans have adopted this time of year for one of their Sabbats. The church calls this day Candlemas and it was considered the first day on which it was possible to do a day's work without needing to light candles.

There is an old saying: 'If Candlemas dawns bright and clear, there will be two winters in that year. If Candlemas is wet and grey the winter's gone and will stay away.' If it is dry and bright there will still be cold weather to come, but if it is raining the bitter frosts have finished. Similarly, with the American 'Groundhog Day', it is said that if this animal appears from its winter hibernation and can see its shadow, it will go back to bed, because there is still cold weather to come.

As the days lengthen, the Wheel of Time returns to the Spring Equinox. This is when day and night are equal, and it is a moment of balance. The Spring Equinox marks the old time for sowing wheat, and in witchcraft, developing ideas for the year of work to come. It is good for planning tasks to perform and skills to master. Also, plants are starting to grow so sources of herbs and medicinal trees are studied as their leaves emerge.

As the seasons turned, from the Spring Equinox towards the greening of early summer, there came the time when animals were moved up to their higher pastures. Sometimes bonfires were lit and the animals symbolically purified by being driven through the smoke of burning herbs. By seeing when the hawthorn starts to bloom you can recognize that summer is on its way, but the dates of the flowering of plants and the ripening of corn are in the hands of Mother Nature herself. In some communities there are processions and dances at this time, celebrating the overcoming of the dark and cold of winter by the light and warmth of the sun. In many parts of Britain there used to be Maypole dances when a ship's mast or tall tree was decked with long ribbons and the young girls and boys wove a variety of patterns as they skipped in and out of each other round the pole. This is thought by some writers to be a really ancient ritual which unites the Earth with the Sky in a kind of wedding, so that their powers are mingled, but there are no really old records of this being so. In some Scandinavian countries tall trees or poles are decked out in flowers or ribbons to drive away the cold of winter.

At midsummer, when the sun stands still again, many hilltops blazed with fiery beacons or bonfires, and in some places quite elaborate public ceremonies were established to celebrate the time of the shortest night. For many years the Druid Orders, which were re-established in the early 1700s, have held gatherings on sacred hilltops or ancient monuments, including Stonehenge and Avebury, to welcome the midsummer sunrise, and reconnect to the tides of Earth and Sky. By marking out a ritual space, offering symbols of the elements of Earth and Water, Fire and Air, they feel they are repeating a symbolic format of considerable antiquity. In Cornwall bonfires are traditionally lit on many high points and on some of these, bunches of flowers and bundles of weeds are cast into the flames by local young women acting as priestesses with a tame sacrifice to ensure bountiful harvest of land and sea. Sheep were shorn later in the year than they are now and a white harvest of their fleeces would be gathered by the shepherds.

In the old days in Britain, the corn would begin to ripen in July and be cut about the beginning of August though now with different strains of grain the harvest may be earlier. The weather still plays a significant part in the timing of this work, for the grain needs to be both ripe and dry when it is gathered, otherwise it will rot. Farmers may have developed different breeds of animals and new species of plants, but while Mother Nature rules the weather, they will still need to watch her moods, and act to her timetable if they want to get the best from their land. This harvest festival is called Lammas from the Saxon words 'Hloaf-mas' meaning a time when new flour may be ground to make bread from this year's corn. It is a time of great concern, as in earlier ages a dearth of flour meant hungry if not starving people, whose diet consisted largely of bread. Customs surround the cutting of the last stalks of corn, the carrying of the stooks into the barns and the grinding of the new flour, in many parts of the world. In Britain, stems of wheat and other grain were saved and woven into corn dollies or kern kings. Many regions had traditional shapes like cornucopias or horseshoes, bound with red ribbons, and these were displayed in the centre of the houses, over the hearth, until the spring sowing when they were mixed into the new seed, to bring a continuity of magic.

The autumn equinox marks the end of summer, and as the nights drew in tasks included finding ways to gather and preserve all the harvests from field and hedgerow, from orchard and vineyard, and secure everything from the winter storms to come. Again the equinox brings a time of balance but now the year is tilting towards winter, with its long nights. There is a Feast of Michaelmas which reflects some of this season's activities, as the Sun symbolically moves into the Sign of Libra. Goose fairs were held when geese with their feet dipped in tar and grit to make boots, were walked to markets, to be fattened for Yule or Christmas. Meat was an important part of the diet of many people, who survived much of the year on smoked hams and bacon, rabbits and pigeons. Red meat was rare for country folk, as it was expensive, and even the chickens which most of us eat regularly were a rare delicacy fifty years ago, roasted for Christmas lunch or at Easter. They were usually only killed when their laying days were over, so they were larger and, if cooked slowly with lots of vegetables and herbs, much more tasty.

In some areas pigs were a vital part of the home economy, fed on scraps as a sort of cleaning up system, and acorns, grass, roots and anything else edible. A fattened pig would be killed at the beginning of winter when the first frosts formed. Much of the pig's meat would be preserved in salt as bacon, or smoked, turned into sausages, brawn and other long-lasting food-stuffs. Some parts had to be eaten at once and a feast was shared by the family to whom the pig belonged. Some of this probably formed part of the Feast of Hallowe'en, at Samhain, meaning 'summer's end'. This was a critical time for people who were so closely connected with the produce of the land. If the crops had been poor, or the summer cool or wet so that little grain could be dried and stored, many people underwent fear and stress which makes our worries pale into insignificance. If Mother Nature had not blessed them, they could starve, or might spend a bitter winter with little to sustain them when their cupboards ran bare.

To many people this was a time when ghosts walked, and prayers for a brighter future would be fervently sent up. Many of the customs which

survive now concern seeing into the future, although the Victorians seem to
have focused these divinations on possible marriage partners. For example,
an apple was peeled with the skin in one piece and this skin was thrown over
the left shoulder. It was supposed to land in the form of the first letter of
a future husband or wife's name. Lots of them must have begun with 'S'!
Probably those who were skilled in far seeing were much more concerned
with the prospects for a warm and dry winter than with who might marry
whom. As the nights grew longer and colder, it was the time for storytelling,
when the traditional legends would be rehearsed around the fire, and the old
myths of life and death, of local heroes and strange monsters would be retold
to a thrilled audience.

There are records of the start of winter being a time when country folk
would gather, light bonfires to lead the spirits of the dead members of
the family to the fireside, or welcome the souls of children to be born into
the household to their new relatives' homes. It was and still is a time of
magic, especially when there are clear frosty nights when every star dazzles
like a diamond on a black velvet sky, and the slender silver crescent of the
moon casts purple shadows on the frozen grass. Here you really do feel that
you can call upon your ancestors and reaffirm the links of family that go
back through the mists of time, joining folk and land, people and tradition
and witch with magic.

Today's Hallowe'en parties with fancy dress and faces painted the spooky
colours of orange, black and green, with witch masks, tales of wizards and
strange-looking food, aren't really the same as the earlier rites which may
have welcomed the ruler of winter. 'Trick or Treat' journeys around the local
community, based on an old Scottish tradition, are part of an old way of
wreaking vengeance, in a small way, on those who have annoyed you during
the year. People would put their clothes on inside out or back to front as a
disguise or to confuse any ghosts that were wandering abroad, and go into
the fields and mix up different farmers' herds of sheep, or take gates off their
hinges. It was a short time when folk could have fun at their neighbours'
expense, without doing any real harm, and old scores could be settled.

Soon it would be the start of the season of Yule, with the winter solstice,
on the shortest day. It was a sacred time for followers of many religions, both
old and newer, and often celebrated the birth of a divine being, the Mabon or

Star Child, a god like Mithras, or a Saviour like Jesus. Each was a bringer of peace and love to his people, whose birth was marked by miraculous happenings and visits by magical or wise men. Many of the customs associated with Christmas have older roots, especially those relating to trees. In the middle ages a huge tree root would be burned on the hearth during the midwinter festival, kindled by the remainder of the previous year's tree. It would burn for the Twelve Days of Yuletide, day and night, so the larger and tougher the better. A small piece would be saved to start next year's fire. This demonstrated a continuity of life from the deep of one midwinter to the next, and the ashes from this burned log were sprinkled on the land to make it fertile.

You will have to start to be aware of the turning seasons wherever you are. If you have a garden, or farmlands or parks nearby, you can start to note when the first flowers appear, when the trees begin to show leaves, and which kind of tree was earliest. You can watch the appearance of birds, butterflies and animals, always being careful not to stop them feeding or drinking. You will soon be amazed at what you discover, especially if you are not used to observing wild creatures. There will be a lot to see, from the minute spears of new green grass to huge trees spreading their summer canopy in a matter of days. If you can look at swathes of countryside you will see a tide of new growth unfold up the hillsides like a rolled-out emerald carpet, or verdant flames climb up each tree in a forest as the new leaves unfold. Watch throughout the whole cycle, and you will see how important these can be to magic. All life is cyclic, being born, developing, mating, growing old and declining to death and rebirth. In magic this circle of being is marked by a long series of repeating sacred dates.

One of the first practical skills you may feel the need to explore is the marking of sacred space. There are many ways of doing this, depending on where you are in the world, what culture has taught you, and what system or tradition of magic you want to follow, but some basic ideas are shared across many traditions, and through many centuries of time. One of these is acknowledging the four directions or points of the compass. You will need to obtain a simple magnetic compass as a useful tool for your magic. It needs only show the basic directions, although if you intend to wander through uncharted country, a more elaborate instrument could be appropriate. Get used to using this by seeing which direction your home faces, where the sun is setting today, where the moon rises the next time you see her. Learn which directions lie around the circle, in the order North, East, South and West. Begin to consider which elements seem most important to each direction, or in what way they are associated in the tradition you are working with.

If you don't already have associations, one fairly common alignment is to place Earth, midnight and winter in the North; Air, sunrise and spring in the East; Fire, noon and midsummer in the South; Water, sunset and autumn in the West; and Light, a globe, timelessness and the stars in the centre. This is not carved in stone, and different ancient cultures have their own ways of aligning the elements. If you are working with any layout, see if it makes sense and, if it is an inherited one, try to understand the significance of placing the elements or other symbols thoroughly. Magical work is about knowledge not dogma or some one else's rules. Learn this, try it, meditate on it and if you feel at peace, use it. If you aren't comfortable look elsewhere for guidance.

Take out your compass and discover where North is, and to mark that find a stone or piece of wood or anything else with the nature of earth. Find the East of your space, and signify it with something of the air, a feather, a scented joss stick or burning incense or a sweet toned bell. Turn to the South and acknowledge the living power of fire, a lighted candle or lamp, a red or yellow flower or anything else you can safely use. Find the West and place a bowl of spring or mineral water or even clean rain water there. Go to the centre of your space and acknowledge your own power, as the centre of that special place, and state silently or out loud your purpose for wishing to make that time and that place sacred.

Be still for a few moments, then go to the North and, in your own words, ask for the strength, stability and stillness of Earth in your work. Carry your stone around in a clockwise circle to mark out the sacred space then replace in its position in the North. Next go to the East and breathe deeply, asking for inspiration and calmness from the Air. Carry the smoking incense or joss stick to mark out the circle. Go to the South and carefully acknowledge the power of Fire, as energy, warmth and courage, again carrying the flame around the sacred space. Go to the West and lift up the water bowl, perhaps dipping your fingers in it to sprinkle upon yourself, saying it will purify your intention, wash away cares and bless the sacred space, as you walk around the circle with it. Lastly, go to the centre and touch the ground, then reach up, asking that from the depths of the Earth to the heights of heaven your magic may be pure, successful, powerful and right. Be still for a few moments, feeling the space reaching out all around you and enclosing you in a bubble of protection and magic.

Within this space, as your knowledge develops, you can perform seasonal celebrations, read Tarot cards, find ways of healing or work on all the witches' crafts in a most effective way. When you have completed your meditation or other work, you will need to release the powers of the elements back into their natural state. Starting with the West give thanks to the purifying power of water and walk a circle with it anticlockwise or widdershins. Then go to the South, carry the fire around, giving thanks for the increase in your own energy and power. Go to the East and walk round scenting the circle widdershins, giving thanks for any inspiration received or to come. Go to the North, take your stone around, saying thank you to the underlying ground, which keeps you safe and secure inside the magical circle and in the world. Finally go to the centre and give thanks for the heights to which you aspire, and the depths from which you draw power. Acknowledge that you are yourself, and a valid and useful human being, who is learning the old arts to help others. Put everything away, so that no one can tell you have made a magical circle there. ⌒↠

Develop this very basic circle ritual for yourself and feel its power grow stronger. You can't 'do it wrong', but you can do it badly by not concentrating on what you are doing, or by not understanding your words or actions, especially if you are simply copying them from a book, without meditating on them.

Five

PLANT POWER

... not unto Thee shall we attain unless Thy name be Love. Therefore

by seed and root and stem and bud and leaf and flower and fruit do

we invoke Thee.

Aleister Crowley, 'The Gnostic Mass', *Magic in Theory and Practice*

Many people understand the use of herbs for healing, but plants provide a wealth of materials to make all kinds of magical equipment, from string to boats, from cloth to houses, from dyes to inks, from paper to magical charms. Special foods can be collected from the wild, wines can be made for ritual occasions from fruits and berries, garlands can be woven to mark the passing seasons, and can also be used for making infusions, teas, embrocations, tinctures, balms and potions for healing and helping, once you start to know your local herbs.

Witchcraft consists of a number of practical skills which only work and direct action can make your own. If you want to be a real witch you will have to learn to recognize the raw materials of your Craft, learn how to shape them, and discover the magical arts which turn a stick into a magic wand, or a leaf into a spell for healing. It is too easy to think that by visiting your local New Age emporium, spending lots of money on all sorts of wonderful things, you will become a witch. Witchcraft consists of real knowledge and understanding, a trained mind and the added insights which come from trusting your intuition. No amount of bought equipment, coven initiations and loaded bookshelves will give you those abilities unless you work at them yourself.

One area of knowledge that the ancient witches were famous for was their knowledge of the use of herbs in healing. They were also associated with the besom, that simple broom made of natural woodland produce. The handle was cut from a hedge – usually hazel or ash – the bristles were clumps of young birch twigs, and it was bound with willow withies. The birch grows in cool, damp areas and is often seen as a weed among trees, so cutting it back to gather the twigs was helping to clear land for cattle. Willows grow near water, and their young shoots are strong and flexible. It is possible that the name witch, and its modern counterpart, wicca, came from the same root word as wicker, meaning withies, which were used to make baskets. It seems to indicate something bent, entwined or woven, or a crooked way rather than a straight one. Perhaps wicker and wicca are actually related, although wicca should be pronounced witcha!

Other plant materials were used to construct walking staffs, sometimes called stangs, which had a fork at the top. Often, they were made from hazel, a magical tree whose twigs are used for dowsing wands, or from ash, which was used for tool handles as it doesn't snap easily. If you are able to work your magic out of doors such a stang may be used as an altar, for it can be pushed into the ground to stand upright, and is easy to decorate with twined ivy, garlands of flowers or ribbons. A shorter wand is used to direct magical power, mark out a circle or stir your potions in the cauldron. This was traditionally made of wood from a nut tree, often hazel or almond, and is as long as your forearm, from fingertip to elbow. It should be straight, and may be carved, painted or simply dried, and perhaps rubbed with beeswax to preserve the wood. It should not have crystals attached to it as these often have a sad and unpleasant history.

If you come across a slice cut from a tree it can be used as an altar top, or to make a talisman. Wood can be made into a box or chest to keep all your magical equipment away from prying eyes, and smaller ones can be designed to hold Tarot cards and other magical items. It is a wonderful material, easy to work, readily available all over the world, and every kind of tree has its own story to tell. Each one traditionally was used for particular jobs: some, like chestnut, were made into fences; alder, whose twigs and bark give four coloured dyes, was used for the piles under bridges as water preserved it. Some of the oldest wooden objects in Britain are the planks and supports of the 'Sweet Track', a stone-age causeway built through marshes near Glastonbury in Somerset. That is made of alder trunks.

Boats were made of pitch pine, larch or oak, and the smaller, ancient coracles were woven like a basket from hazel and willow and originally covered with skins, although similar modern boats have tarred fabric coverings. Houses were made of wattles, which are split and woven hazel poles, covered with daub made of mud or clay, and larger buildings were prefabricated from the great limbs of oak trees, whose curves matched the shape of the roof. All these aspects of woodworking would have been familiar to our ancestors, who may have lived in round wattle and daub houses, marking their magical circles on the bare earth floor with a patch swept by a besom. They would have sat on benches or chairs carved from local hardwoods, eaten off wooden platters, used all kinds of farming implements and magical tools shaped from different kinds of timber. Even the firewood would have been chosen carefully for its slow-burning and heat-producing properties.

Life is too easy these days, with shops full of goodies, markets filled with a wide variety of foods and fruits which, left to Mother Nature, we would taste only in season, or by visiting far-off places. We also have our occult needs pandered to, with ready-made robes, instant incense, and pre-consecrated ritual gear of all sorts, as well as books explaining spells in words of one syllable. Some modern covens have forgotten about the actual processes of crafting candles, sewing robes, baking ritual cakes, blending incenses – all this has been set aside in favour of shopping!

In the old days people had to make everything because they couldn't just buy it, and there was real pride in the construction of useful or beautiful items, whether to be eaten or used for many years. Today there are plenty of good and useful books which give instructions on the crafts of making various items, but many people are just too tied up to set aside the time from work, play, watching TV or any of the other distractions of modern life. Anyone who has made the effort to create something is not 'wasting time' in its manufacture, but is offering love, effort, concentration, to Mother Nature who provides the materials, and the Lord of Learning who strengthens your skill.

A first area of knowledge which we know goes right back through the history of humanity, and which still forms an essential plank in the works of witchcraft is the use of plant power. It may be obvious that some plants can be eaten cooked or raw in salads, others may offer fruits which can be turned into drinks, for example wine from grapes, but there is a lot more to it than that. Every land has its tradition of herbal medicines, where leaves, roots, stems, buds, flowers and juices have been used for thousands of years to help cure all manner of diseases. A lot of this knowledge was forgotten, especially with the rise of interest in chemicals and artificial drugs made by industrial processes. Much of the healing work was in the hands of the women and menfolk in the villages, who did their best to help people and animals with traditional plant remedies. Then this power was taken over by pharmaceutical companies and their industrial-sized profits. The herbalists were scorned and their ancient knowledge devalued and thought to be ignorant rubbish.

A revival of this idea is happening now, as the old cures are being reexamined and found to be effective, for example St John's Wort (Hypericum), in cases of depression. As rainforests are being cut down and their trees and plants destroyed scientists are discovering what the local people knew for thousands of years, that these areas can provide cures for many serious illnesses. It is almost too late, but it really is important that anyone who wants to call themselves a witch should be aware of the many valuable properties of plants. It is easy to learn the names and uses of trees and leaves and flowers when you are a child, especially if you grow up in the countryside, with wild plants all around you, but as an adult, trying to recall the names and properties of hundreds of different plants and herbs is much harder. Ideally, you will need a wise companion who really can recognize each plant which grows in your region, and tell you its uses and how it should be prepared.

In Britain we are fortunate to have thousands of medicinal plants growing, often wild, all over the country, but learning about them is still difficult. There are several schools of herbal medicine, and in many places there are evening classes or day schools which introduce interested people to trees, herbs or fungi, and though this may only be superficial, it can be a valuable start. At such classes you might well meet up with more experienced people who can help you learn, or several of you might be trainee witches, and can work together. Although it is best not to clutter your home with too many books of spells and incantations, really good herbals or plant identifying books with photographs or clear illustrations are essential. Certainly, you can buy many herbs dried and prepared by experts, and for some purposes these may be ideal, but many common medicinal and culinary plants can easily be grown, even in a windowbox or very small patch of earth. Most cities have a botanical garden or herb collection you can visit, and these places also run identification talks, or lectures by experts on their collections. Do a bit of basic research, for even garden centres, where you might go to stock up your own plot, will have knowledgeable people on hand to explain about the different herbs and fruit trees.

Plant matter is an essential raw material for magic. They can be eaten, like the sacred cakes for festivals which can be made of wheat flour, or ground almonds, or oats, with added dried fruits, spices and sugar, all of which come from plants. You might drink grape wine or, ideally, make your own from local fruits and even vegetables, if you want to add that witchy skill to your Crafts. Ideas for festival food can be found in many books, or your own favourite recipes may be adapted by adding things which link you to the season, for example, in the autumn you can add nuts or fresh fruits which you have gathered. If you prefer to have a celebration meal you can get to know what regional specialities and what seasonal vegetables are to be had, perhaps in a farmers' market. Knowing what is in season and what is produced locally is another way of linking with your own aspect of Mother Nature, for all foods and fruits are her gifts.

If you really feel drawn to see the Earth Mother and the Lord of the Sky as deities who you personally want to worship, communicate with or honour, you can use your growing knowledge of the natural world as your own religious practice. There are no rules for today's pagans, only what each holds to be true from experience. The practical use of Crafts can be seen as prayers, for they are ways of bonding with the eternal deities, showing respect, honour and love. We have cut the spiritual dimension out of our lives because we only meet for seasonal feasts or to work some spell at the full moon. That is not enough. Followers of other faiths give more – Moslems pray five times every day, Christians may well go to church at least once every week, so why should pagans do less for their chosen gods and goddesses. Do you pray five times a day, or set aside hours every Sunday to worship, making acts of thanksgiving or petitions? Don't your goddesses and gods warrant that amount of attention? Don't they need your thanks, your requests, your worship?

Prayer doesn't have to be on your knees or flat on your face, it can take the form of work. It can be the slow sewing of the seams of a robe by hand, it can be the preparing, drying and blending of woods, flowers and gums for incense, it can be the digging of a new garden plot, the planting of bulbs for spring, the pruning of roses for next summer. All these can become acts of worship and thanksgiving. Turn your mind to working for the powers of Nature, asking their help with a hard or heavy task, asking their patience if it takes ages to get it right. If you begin to work for them in every act you make, then all your life becomes worship. It isn't enough to think about it, or speak about it, it is a matter of engaging your heart, and so making it real.

What joy is to be gained by getting someone else to do your work for you? Are you so useless that you can't seek out a straight growing hazel switch or the branch of a willow to make a wand. Cut it with care and love, allow it to dry straight and tall, carve it, shape it, or merely complete Mother Nature's work by polishing it with wax and turpentine, both natural, sweet-smelling and preservative, giving wood a golden gleam. You don't need to visit psychic fairs and pay someone else a lot of money for an alien stick, no matter how pretty and covered in carvings and crystals from some foreign land. Look for yourself when workers are cutting hedges or when trees are pruned, or there is something in your own neighbourhood that can be cleanly cut and used for magic.

Can you not find a strip of cloth, ideally organic cotton or linen, both plant fibres, or even hemp cloth or natural wool or silk from a good supplier? It only needs to be a little wider than your shoulders and reach down to your ankles, and have a hole to put your head through. A simple coloured cord around it is all you need to make a ritual robe or simple kaftan. Are you so unwilling to make a bit of effort on behalf of those mighty beings which gave you all you consider to be yours, to find the time to visit a library or bookshop and find patterns for tunics, gowns and more elaborate garments which are easy and quick to make? Having a special robe for magic helps to change you into a magical person. Its putting on and taking off focus you on the work or meditation in hand. It sets that part of your life apart from the everyday affairs, so long as you respect your robes, wear them only for magical activities and keep them clean and neat.

All the things important in Craft magic can be made, remade or developed by anyone who calls her- or himself a witch. Some writers go on at length about special knives called athames but there is no history of such an instrument outside modern books. None of the witch trials mention convicting people on the strength of having a special knife or cauldron or broomstick, as everyone had these things. If you must have a special knife, go and find an old carving knife in a kitchen drawer, or ask a grandmother to see if she has a well-worn steel knife you can adapt. You can reshape the blade, sharpen it, make a new hilt out of wood or horn and, as it ought to be sharp, make a scabbard for it out of leather, if you are traditional (recycle an old handbag or a jacket), or wood and metal if you prefer.

Pentacles or platters, as symbols of Elemental Earth, can be made of wood, for example an old breadboard or a slice of tree polished and carved, or slabs of natural stone, bits of marble washstands or slate dug out of hedges – use your imagination, your inner guidance and craftiness to make something to use. Cups can be modelled from clay or you can attend pottery classes and make more enduring ones. You can swap something you have made for something someone else has made, for bartering skills, knowledge or abilities was always the way that Craftsfolk lived. They would exchange their magic, divination powers or healing skill for food, clothing or useful materials. Candles may be made from beeswax, which is usually a by-product of honey production, or you can reuse old ends, or buy some wax to blend with other wax from this source. You will need wicks and moulds, but the Craft can be gained with ingenuity.

Another use for natural products is in making your own book of records. You can get wonderful handmade paper, again made from wood pulp and other natural fibres, and learn how to bind it, using old methods if you wish. Making such a volume is another craft you can master. You may want to start to collect poems, prayers, spells and rituals and it is best to write down the words in your own handwriting. This ensures that you at least look at the words, and try to understand them as they are carefully copied out in your best handwriting. It is too easy to rely on a computer printer or photocopier – what joy or skill is there in that? What beneficial use do you put the time saved to? Not studying what you have copied mechanically. When things were done slowly and by hand, they sunk into the depths of consciousness gently, where they would always dwell, ready for use at a moment's notice.

That is what Craftsmanship is about – knowledge ingrained in heart and eye, so that when a technique is needed you can use it immediately, be it healing, spell making or giving thanks to the Lady who has provided you with the raw materials for something beautiful. Speed is not everything, caring can be. Value all the things that you can make, and expand your skills all the time by learning from others. Share what you can do well freely and gladly in exchange for other knowledge or guidance and the rewards will be enormous and fulfilling.

There are huge collections of books about initiations, festivals, tools, goddesses and gods, ritual procedures, and so on, but there also seems to be quite a list of the things that modern witches don't do, or even know about any more. There are many topics which our ancestors had considerable knowledge about from practical experience, especially if they were ordinary country people. What they learned first and foremost was to be observant and to notice everything that was going on about them. This involved looking at the land each morning and seeing what had come into fruit or flower, to determine the menu for dinner and any decorations inside the house. They would look at the crops and the flowerbeds and the sky as well to determine weather patterns, and at clouds, rain, wind direction and so on, to predict what would happen for the rest of the day. It was also possible to smell the change of seasons, an inexplicable sensation, but real, nonetheless. Anyone can learn to recognize when the air smells of harvest and the reaping of corn.

If you want to use a plant in magic you have to be able to recognize it, but most witches pick their plants from wild places, so you need to be able to recall exactly where in the locality a single plant is growing. This is a mixture of trained memory and intuition, because if there is a choice of sites, some may be showing plants in a better condition than others. It is important not only to recognize plants in their natural habitat, but also to know about the soil beneath your feet. The nature of the ground affects the kinds of plants you can discover, so getting to understand the rock, clay or loam which is in your garden or in any wild or neglected places nearby, where many useful plants or 'simples' may be found, is important. Look at the trees, some will grow well on chalk, like beeches and yews, others prefer more acid soils or clay, like hazels and oaks. Get to know your trees, they each give off a kind of aura of energy which can easily be used. They endure much longer lives than humans, and recent scientific developments have established, through the patterns of trees' growth rings, the weather in many parts of the world, over thousands of years. Like us they grow, mature, have offspring, and eventually die, but continue through their seeds and nuts. Planting trees is a true way of leaving an inheritance for the future.

If you are feeling tired or stressed, if you need reassurance that your magical skills will develop, you might benefit from a bit of Tree Power. One exercise you can do, to give you a connection with Mother Nature, is to find a good, strong and healthy tree of a species you recognize, where you can stand or sit at its feet. Take off your shoes if you can, and stand with your back to the tree, straightening your spine as much as you can, and reaching back with your hands behind your hips to clasp the trunk. Stand very still and relax. Listen to any sounds, of wind in the leaves, the movements of small animals, birdsong or the hum of insects. Gradually allow yourself to lean more closely into the tree and feel its strength and support. Feel your feet, and imagine they too have roots, sinking down beside those of the tree, deep into the earth. Feel rooted and secure. As you continue to explore this sensation, imagine a honey-like essence of earth energy beginning to flow up through your feet. Feel it, like warm, smooth syrup, filling you up with a golden source of life energy. Begin to sense the slow way of life of your chosen tree, how days and nights are swift to pass, and that the seasons have a greater impact.

Sense the coldness of a barren winter giving way to the joy of spring sunshine. Feel yourself deeply connected to the Earth, drawing nourishment from it, and being made stronger and more in control. Allow your senses to spread like summer leaves, blossom like sweet flowers, reach out around you like long branches moved by a gentle summer wind. Feel the development of your seeds, fruits or nuts and the release as they fall to earth, or are carried away by birds or animals. Feel all the living things around you, the butterflies and moths, the squirrels and all the birds that roost or feed among your leaves. Sense those qualities which trees have that you miss in your own life: the ability to endure through rain and storm; the patience to wait for the coming of spring; the slow change and growth to being a mighty supporter of situations around you.

As you continue to allow these images and feelings to flow through you, begin to notice a different, light, sparkling energy which falls upon you like the softest raindrops. See this as solar light, the other source from which living things are nourished. Feel warmth but also a dynamic, fizzing energy, which shifts through rainbow colours, tingling down from the top of your head to your toes. Sense this being drawn in with every breath you take, permitting life force and healing to be absorbed, right through you. Allow this to drive out any negative feelings you may have, or fears and doubts. Fill up with both aspects of tree force, the slow enduring earth honey and the bright, sparkling solar energy, until they flow from your finger tips and toes and the top of your head in radiant showers of living light. Remain poised and fully aware of these experiences, and then let them drain away down through your feet to the earth.

You should feel fully revived by this experience, and it may help you to align yourself with the ancient energy of Nature. Try the same thing with different kinds of trees, and you will find that some will seem to dance lightly upon the earth, while others are sunk deep, solid and unmoving even in tempests. Some will feel friendly and will welcome you to share their nourishments, while others, if they have been cruelly treated by people, will be less sympathetic. Maybe you can offer apologies to them, or some kind of relief from what is harming them. You can always make an offering of rainwater with some plant food in it as a thank you. Pour this in a circle a pace or so away from the tree's trunk, as that is where the most active roots will be. This can be an incredibly healing and uplifting experience, if it is done with honour and intent, for trees have been closely associated with human development from very early times.

Of course smaller plants, herbs and shrubs also offer the witch all kinds of useful materials. If you want to start making potions to drink, or use plants in ointments, wines or in any other way, you need to know exactly what you are dealing with. Many common garden plants are poisonous and though their flowers might look pretty as decoration on a salad, they can make you ill. It is probably best to start with a few of the common culinary herbs, if you want to use the old art of 'wort cunning' or herbal witchcraft. You may already grow some very useful healing plants in your garden or can easily get them from a plant supplier. Herbs like thyme, which is very good in soups and stews, is an excellent way to soothe a sore throat. Take about two teaspoonfuls of fresh leaves (or one if you have to use dried thyme), and put it into a heat-proof jug. Pour about half a pint of boiling water over these leaves and allow it to steep for at least five minutes, or until the liquid is cool enough to drink. Filter the liquid into a clean bottle and sip a little every few hours to soothe a sore throat or help heal mouth ulcers. The cooled infusion may be stored in the fridge for a few days. You may just gargle with this if you don't like the taste, or add a little honey, ideally whilst the liquid is still warm.

Similar teas or tisanes may be made from the culinary varieties of sage as this is very soothing to sore gums or inflamed tonsils. Basil may be made into an infusion and drunk to ease mild indigestion or, whilst the leaves are soaking in the hot water, the steam may be inhaled to ease blocked sinuses or tension headaches which start over the eyes. Another infusion is made from the wild herb goosegrass, or cleavers, which has clinging stems of bright green and tiny white flowers in the summer. A handful of the fresh stems and leaves with about a pint of boiling water poured over them should be left to steep for five to ten minutes. The liquid should be strained into a jug and small cups drunk to counteract the effects of rich food or heavy meals. Leaves and stems of rosemary may be prepared in the same way and the resulting infusion used as a rinse for dark hair, after it has been shampooed. Drinking diluted rosemary tea is supposed to assist the memory, and can awaken psychic skills involving forgotten information in witches.

Other common plants which offer simple herbal remedies for minor ills include marigolds, whose petals are soaked in hot water and then cooled to refresh tired eyes. The petals crushed into a basic hand cream or even Vaseline will make a useful emollient for dry skin and small cuts and scratches, especially those received while gardening. Marigold tea is thought to help counteract yeast infections, although it is necessary to adjust your diet if you have candida or other 'thrush-like' disorders. Fresh parsley is very rich in iron and, when chopped and added to salads and soups, or simply scattered over cooked vegetables every day, can help keep infections at bay, as will eating young dandelion leaves. If you have this apparent weed in your garden, as many witches do, recognize it has many uses. If a plant is covered with a flowerpot the leaves will blanch like expensive endive, and can be eaten raw in salads. When the plant flowers, the white latex juice squeezed from a cut flower or leaf stem onto a wart will help kill the virus. You could also chant a spell, 'Dandelion, bright and sure, make my skin clean and pure. White juice from your heart, make my blemishes depart. As it darkens, day by day, make my warts all melt away.' Touch a new juicy stem to the wart each day during the waning half of a moon and you will gain surprising relief. You have to leave the dark staining juice on the wart and surrounding area each time so that it can work effectively.

Today many people make use of aromatherapy oils, and many of these can be very useful. To make your own you will need to use either almond or grapeseed oil as a base, and then crush into it as many clean flowers of a particular plant as you can. The best to experiment with include white jasmine, lavender or rose petals. If the petals are crushed and placed in a jar of oil with an airtight lid and stood in a dim warm place for a few days the scent will infuse into the oil. It won't be as strong as commercial aromatherapy oils as they have their scents extracted by steam or other industrial processes, but for ritual use this is fine. After a few days, depending on conditions, strain the liquid through a fine sieve into a clean bottle, label it, and place it in the dark. These oils may be used sparingly for anointing before magical work or, if you get enough of a scent, burned on an oil burner for perfume. Otherwise they could be added to a warm bath for relaxation and sweet dreams.

Plants will teach you their qualities, as will animals, birds and natural events if you can shut off the modern rational conceptions about the meaning of learning. Books should not be seen as the only teachers, but as many of us have lost our inherited knowledge of plants, their identifications, methods of preservations, storage and use, well-illustrated modern herbals are a great aid. Books can help us, because we have forgotten to use other methods, but our ancestors did not keep records of learning, they gained it through observation and copying their older family members. They asked trees for information, they watched the sky for weather lore, they saw animals as predictors of change. The witch's familiar was not a pet, but a genuine helper, in this realm and many others, to guide and inform.

Not only do witches use plant leaves, flowers and fruits for magical processes, they also spin thread from a variety of plant materials. One of the most beautiful is that made from the stalks of stinging nettles. These plants grow all over the place, and at the end of the summer when the stems are tall they may be cut and 'retted', which means soaking them in running water to wash away the green parts. They are then dried and scraped of any excess material, and the fibres combed out. This produces a golden silk-like thread which may be spun, woven or even knitted. There are all sorts of ancient and magical uses for string, cord and thread. Even basic knots like the much maligned 'Granny Knot' have a use in magic, as do the reef, clove hitch, surgeon's knot and noose, for each may be used to fasten together the red thread of a spell, to make a tripod to suspend the cauldron over the fire, to spellbind and to create hitches in the web of life.

There are lots of spells which involve things being untied, for instance when a woman or animal is in labour – every cord and binding in the area is loosened to help the process along. However, if something has to be bound, be it time or an action, the right-coloured wool spirally wound the right number of turns will help the spell along. 'Cats Cradle' is a string game found all over the world, and is used by sorcerers and shamans of the old school, for the interaction of the two participants making the nets, meshes and patterns between their hands is a memory aid for recalling a magical tale or chant. Nets, too, were used in magic, to control certain kinds of spirits. Nets made of spider's webs are used for scrying in Hallowe'en games. Cords and the knots in them formed a kind of ancient pagan rosary from which certain old spells were recalled and remembered. Tying a knot in a strip of paper will reveal one of the witches' oldest secrets, explaining much to those who have the eyes to see, and answer a mathematical puzzle.

Always be on the lookout for unusual and neglected places where wild plants may be found. At first you will simply need to learn to recognize what grows where, and from a good book or better still a real teacher, discover the powers, uses and effects of the many plant products around you. For example, hedges are places of great value. A vast number of healing herbs and awakening plants are to be found in the hedgerows. Study the plants which make up a hedge – the older the hedge the more species of trees and shrubs. Some date back to the first enclosures, in Merlin's day! Most are full of useful berries, seeds, hips and haws for food and comfort. Many are homes to small animals and birds of all kinds. Make a bottle of plant food of rain or spring water and offer it at the foot of any wild hedge. Use this to pay for hazel dowsing rods, the ash wand, the blackthorn walking stick and the magic stang.

Hedges are great teachers, and cutting them can be a valuable asset to meditation, if you do it with shears, not an electric cutter. Find your own mental and spiritual boundaries and then create beautiful gates revealing a way through to new worlds beyond. Think of the plants as Gatekeepers to the Other Worlds, who will take you by the hand and gently lead you through, to power, to beauty, to all the magical landscapes which exist in other realms, cut off only by an ancient hedge. Be prepared to make notes, gather samples for later identification, or for pressing into your own personal plant collection record.

Trees, herbs, flowers, leaves, roots, stems, seeds, buds and fibres all have their place in the old magics of the witches, and it is a life-time's study to know them all. Even fungi were used to produce visions when used properly by the shamans of Siberia and the far North. Poisonous plants and seeds were used to kill vermin, or in smaller doses, mixed with fat, made into Flying Ointment, which when rubbed into the skin gave out-of-body experiences. Witches knew exactly how to blend these deadly juices to give deep sleep or pain relief, or even death to the old, injured and infirm. It was for this knowledge that they may have been feared, but you have to accept that every part of life can have its dangers. Knowing that you could kill someone with your car in a moment of inattention seldom stops you driving. Some plants, even medicinal herbs in the wrong doses, can be dangerous, but if you are careful, working from safe, ordinary culinary herbs towards the wild plants and their potent effects, you can gain a great insight into the work of the old witches, and offer healing and help to those around you.

If you really want to master the Crafts of old magic you will have to develop a whole range of almost forgotten skills. You can learn to make garlands of flowers to deck your sacred place, you can scent candles with sweet flowers, you can blend incenses of gums and resins and dried wood shaving from special trees. You can learn to talk to trees and use their twigs for divination, or cut hazel wands to use as dowsing rods. You can brew teas and potions, learn to make alcoholic tinctures, ointments, simples, and all the skills of wort-cunning. You can carve pieces of timber into magical boxes or altar tops, you can build furniture, spin cord, weave linen threads into cloth or dye it with plant colours. You can cast spells or make charms from branches of sacred trees, drive out harm with magical rowan wands, eat fruits, smell flowers, drink the juices and dozens more things all from Mother Nature's gifts of trees and herbs, for these are the raw materials of witchcraft, not complicated rituals set out in books, or the worship of imported gods and goddesses. These are the real essentials of the Craft, and knowing their use and the ancient wisdom they offer is what it is all about.

Six

LINKING WITH THE LANDSCAPE

There is a pleasure in the pathless wood,

There is a rapture in the lonely shore,

There is society where none intrudes,

By the deep sea, and Music in its roar.

I love not Man the less, but Nature more.

Lord Byron, 'Childe Harold's Pilgrimage'

Witchcraft is a magical tradition which has deep roots in the ground and all that grows upon it. Almost every land had people with special powers, in each community or tribe. In some areas these individuals were known as shamans, and their work was concerned with reaching beyond the limits of life to retrieve the damaged souls of sick people. To become a shaman was not by initiation or teaching but by undergoing some life-threatening experience which took the shaman beyond the ordinary world into the realm of spirits. There he or she would make allies with otherworldly beings who could assist in curing the sick, or restoring the mentally ill to health. Only by a personal connection to the spirit world, achieved by what we might call an 'out-of-body experience' or 'near-death experience' were the powers to be a shaman given to the newcomer.

Often these special people suffered long and debilitating illnesses, taking them to the very edge of the land of the dead before they were able to recognize what was happening and, by taking on the work of shamanism, find their cure. Because of this they were then able to cure others. Later on, the Northern shamans of Siberia were associated with the use of special herbs or fungi which gave them the ability to travel in a spirit boat or fly with magical birds to the realm beyond the shores of death, to gain help for the sick. They also used drumming which is not a natural part of every tradition.

Some people believe they can simply become shamans by going to a weekend workshop, banging on a drum or bodhran, dancing around a bit and decorating their homes with foreign symbols. Similarly, some folk feel that they can easily become witches with the powers to connect to Mother earth, work with the energies of Nature, heal with herbs, scry in a black mirror or perform any of the other battery of folk magics which take a lifetime to learn. You can't buy or trade for or be given the ancient skills of mind and hand except by earning these for yourself through hard and enduring work.

The ancient magic workers drew a certain amount of their power from the land they lived in, and that is where newcomers will need to look to find places where they can reconnect to it in their own region. There have always been special places which we might call sacred, which have been fenced off or marked with a natural source of energy, a pure spring of water, for example, or the highest peak of a hill or mountain, where earth and sky meet. In many lands certain great trees were holy, either sheltering a great teacher, as the Bodhi Tree sheltered Buddha, or, like the Tree of Life, symbolizing knowledge in a more abstract way. In ancient Egypt the body of the god, Osiris, was placed inside a hollow sycamore tree, and in Britain many significant and religious events took place under the dark canopy of immortal yew trees.

Nature herself indicates her sacred sites by what is put there through time. Free-standing rocks, often carved by time into faces or god-like shapes, were thought to be holy places. Deep caves were not only retreats for humans from the weather and wild animals, but also, through painted or chipped decoration, temples and dwelling places of the immortals. In many parts of the world there are sacred springs, rock overhangs or caves where magical symbols have been marked, often over many generations, where the pictures have been redrawn or enlarged. These kinds of works of magical art are found on many continents, and though we cannot always read the story they tell or decipher the mystery they illustrate we are able to recognize their incredible age, and that they show animals and magic workers who lived long ago. Archaeologists are discovering more and more decorated caves every year, and through dating materials left behind, like seashells used to mix colours, or charcoal, they know these drawings were made many thousands of years ago. If we look at these pictures with the sight of a witch we can often discover that ritual dances, using carved or decorated sticks as wands, or painted symbols that attract success in life, are similar to those we use today.

Every region had its magical hot spots where the inner forces of the Earth welled up and could be used by magicians, or a sacred spring whose water would bring healing. Even now there are spa towns famous for their mineral waters and curative properties, where people can go to bathe or drink from the strange-tasting springs. In antiquity, temples were erected to various gods and goddesses, and for hundreds of years worshippers could offer prayers, bring offerings of flowers or animals, hear oracles, or receive guidance or healing. Some temples were places to sleep in so that your dreams could be interpreted by priestesses, or to immerse yourself in the hot waters of a thermal bath. There was always a reason for the location of sacred places, perhaps because the ancient gods and goddesses had told their followers to raise a temple there, or because some even more ancient natural sign was clearly visible.

We are citizens of a great world, we can travel to places and explore many cultures. We have historians and archaeologists who are revealing more and more about the lives and beliefs of our ancestors, and we can learn about foreign cultures, hear strange languages, visit shrines and temples and ruins where gods used to dwell in ways our forefathers would have thought impossible. We may have access to all this ancient information but unless we really understand it such knowledge is useless. Some critics of the New Age movement have accused its seekers of being able to design 'pick and mix' religions or philosophies, by taking myths from one land, deities from another, ritual practices from a third and ideas from all over the place. Sometimes this is true. However, witchcraft has to be linked to the land you are in now.

It is by creating a personal bond with the earth beneath you and the sky above you that you can discover your own magic.

Witches are those who stand between heaven and earth, drawing on each for magical energies which are bent and shaped by their individual knowledge and Crafts. By looking around you and acknowledging that other people have stood on that place for hundreds, perhaps thousands of years, you are connecting to them in a subtle way. Today's Craft is not about trying to live or think or offer sacrifices as our ancestors did, but to admit we share their beliefs in the unseen realm entered through the dreaming mind. We have the same desires for a secure home, companionship from family or friends, enough to eat, good health and a useful occupation. If we could talk to our Stone-Age cousins their needs would be very similar to ours. The places that many of them marked out as special still exist.

We may not be able to explain how they constructed some of Europe's great monolithic structures, or why they pointed their burial mounds at the midwinter sunrise, but we can honour them through honouring their heritage to us. If we visit those places with open inner eyes and a humble request for knowledge it will come. If we treat their temples with respect, taking nothing but photographs, leaving nothing at all except footprints, we will take with us in our hearts pictures of places to visit in meditation, and to explore through dreams. If we dishonour these sacred sites by leaving candle ends, burying crystals or damaging the subtle and ancient energies by anything we do, we harm not only those special places, holy to many people, but we harm ourselves, by showing what ignorant and unthinking visitors we are. Don't even offer flowers or fruits for their decay can damage delicate plants and lichens which could have taken hundreds of years to grow.

We, who are often world travellers, must remember that the old witches grew up, married, lived and died within quite a small area, drawing on ancestral knowledge from one place. Later records show that they supplemented this with information imported in books, as many were great readers, using early 'mail order' book suppliers. They would know every tree and patch of plants, source of clay or peat or any other useful substance within miles of their homes. Today we get our knowledge from all over the world, in printed or electronic form, but it is no substitute for getting to know your home territory, its history, products, people and plants. Choosing a personal 'patch', be it a street, a village, a garden or a whole town to get to know and love is as essential to a modern witch as it was to her ancestors.

You may come upon people these days who call themselves witches, some of whom wander around festivals and conferences dressed in deepest black with flapping cloaks, resplendent in flowing robes covered in ankhs and pentagrams, and carrying lavishly-carved staffs, but this uniform is not compulsory! Whatever it is they are symbolizing, they seem to have missed the point about Natural Religions. Those who are on the path of the Wildwood are Mother Nature's children, they are closest to her in situations where everything surrounding them is simple. They perceive her in the night sky, rising among the stars as the ever-changing Moon, in the wild places where cultivation has left small areas of rough grazing, spinneys or open moorland.

Here you will be able to listen to the voice of the Earth in the grasses, feel the brush of her garment touching your face in the breeze, sense her presence in the loneliness of a wide sky. She does not demand that people dress up in strange outfits to worship her or seek her presence. She does not request expensive incenses, or strange, and often alien symbols to be worn in her honour. Her blessings are to be encountered in every shower of rain, in every bank of wild flowers, in the restless and varied tones of the streams and deep oceans.

Witchcraft is about continuity, and though it may be true not many people now spend their whole lives in the place where their parents, grandparents and ancestors lived and died, your forebears must have lived somewhere! If you start to look back through family records and old photo albums, and ask your oldest relatives about their jobs, homes and memories, you might be surprised at how much you can learn. If you have access to birth or marriage certificates these often note where people lived and what their occupations were. There aren't likely to be records of people giving their job as 'witch' or 'cunning man', especially as most active folk healers and herbalists worked their magic as a side line to their full-time occupation, but you may uncover a history of country skills.

You may discover, if you can get records going back three or four generations, that your family came from a particular place. You can visit this and possibly locate your ancestors' gravestones in the churchyard. You may wish to turn your back on the teachings of Christianity but you ought to be open-minded enough to honour the old buildings and their encircling gardens. These often show genuine links with an ancient and magical past, and maintain a peaceful atmosphere even in a bustling city or town. Remember, churches were built by craftsmen with their own secrets, and hidden among the carvings are many which can be interpreted as pagan. If you were visiting a foreign place you would probably go to see the temples or museums, the sacred places and monuments of that nation and, even if you didn't really understand their religion or practices, you could enjoy the artwork, the carvings, paintings or coloured glass. If you treat old churches the same way, you will be astonished at what you might discover.

Churches were often built near to earlier sacred structures, be they Roman temples, holy springs, stone circles or high on hilltops where the communities gathered to light bonfires to celebrate special dates. In Britain there are many extremely ancient yew trees, often predating the churches, which have been built among their roots or in their shade, by hundreds, or possibly thousands of years. In other places the circular churchyard wall marks a prehistoric enclosure or the standing stones mark the remains of a barrow or tumulus. Only by visiting these places with an open mind and a sense of recognizing the original sacredness of the land will you start to see how important the place is within the context of its landscape. Look out for the carved faces with twining leaves coming from their mouths, the Green Men and occasional Green Ladies whose exact meaning is forgotten. Look for the hidden cats and deer, the frogs and toads under the seats, the stars and moons and suns gleaming in brilliant-coloured glass in the windows. Few of these are part of the Christian story, yet may be part of a lost legacy to the works of people who lived in that place long ago. If you don't look and try to understand you will never make these startling discoveries for yourself.

Another rich vein of tradition is that of folk custom. This has hardly been examined at all by the followers of wicca, since Gerald Gardner died in the 1960s. Every community had certain special days to celebrate, for example a procession on May day, a dance and gathering or bonfire at midsummer, a party marking a harvest of crops, the beginning of ploughing, blessing the apple trees by Wassailing in January or countless other occasions throughout the land and the year. A bit of basic research will tell you about your local events, but it is the being there, the real, physical experience of the sounds, the smells, the people and their excitement that turns a flat piece of information into a real, valid and living experience. Certainly it is hard to prove these events go back into the depths of history, but that is not always important. The sheer exuberance of participating is really quite magical, and that is why this knowledge is needed.

Those old festivals are part of the wider arts of country magic. If you bless the orchards in the spring, by offering cider to the roots, and fire shotguns through the branches of the apple trees to drive away harm, and if you encourage a pretty young girl to climb up to fix pieces of toast dipped in cider to the branches, who knows what luck you are inviting. The birds will come to eat the bread and perhaps the pests in the trees, cider libations may nourish the production of blossom, the shots may prune the highest branches – who knows, but these old spells may do some practical good too. Every old practice has a whole list of reasons: some are boring everyday ones; others invoke the powers of Nature to bless the orchards, or the standing corn, where it was said that witches leapt over their broomsticks to make the crops grow tall. Magic works with nature, adding an extra dimension to ordinary tasks. No one can say it doesn't do any good, and many customs are thought to go back at least hundreds of years. Magic only survives when it works.

By getting to know every tree, riverside, shrub, park or field in your area you will start to understand how people have interacted with the landscape for generations. Hardly anywhere in Europe is untouched, yet many of the alterations which people made were originally for religious or spiritual reasons. Many high hills had standing stones or earthworks placed upon them. Some were defensive in times of invasion, but others were for the glory of Nature or to connect with the gods of the sky. There is a wonderful experience which anyone can have by reaching the highest place around and lying on the ground and looking up. You can't then see the works of humanity, you can be alone with the sacred energies of the Earth beneath you, and sense the freedom and light of the heavens above. You form a magical link, just as your forebears may have done hundreds of years ago, and from that essential experience you can draw down power to use in your circles and rituals later on.

At night this can be even more wonderful, for if the sky is clear, even the light pollution of a city is blotted out if you are looking to the zenith of the sky at the ribbons of stars, and the brilliance of the planets, which do not twinkle like stars, but glow with a steady, often coloured light. The moon's face shows the myriad patterns of craters, even to your own eyes, but a pair of binoculars will bring out even greater detail. Did you know that the planet Venus, which is the brightest of the planets, has phases like the Moon, or that you can sometimes see the rings of Saturn? From places like planetariums it is possible to buy slides produced by deep space telescopes which show stars and galaxies, comets and nebulae in ways our ancestors might have only observed when out of their bodies. If these are blown up through a projector it is almost like being in the depths of space, but you can voyage in the spirit until you see the Earth as a small blue-green orb, veiled with clouds set in the black sky. You don't need the virtual reality of modern technology for those trained in magic have had spiritual reality since the dawn of time. Teach yourself to really see, whether it is an ant on the grass or the galaxies of the cosmos, and you will awaken real magic in your soul.

By getting to know your neighbourhood and the surrounding area, by looking for peaceful bits of countryside you can explore, and learning the plants and the trees, the fungi and the wildlife by observation, by hearing them, by smelling them, you will begin to renew or build up the old powers of witchcraft. You will find places and times when it is safe for you and perhaps a few friends to go to celebrate your inner work. Try to go out soon after dawn, to perform a ceremony with a magical intent. That is what most witches want to do, and the world is full of secluded or remote places where the wind and sun, the starlight and the breeze and the voices of Nature can be encountered first hand. It is so much more powerful than being inside a building, and answers flow so much more readily. Certainly, it can be scary to be out alone at night, but that is part of the fun. If your heart is not pounding and your senses heightened then you may not gain the insights the goddesses and the gods of the living world can teach you.

You need to learn the basic arts of tuning in, which will not only help your inner vision to clear, but will indicate clearly to you where and when you might expect to encounter the ancient ones. Make a dowsing pendulum with a length of thin cord and a symmetrical object like a large bead, or even a needle and thread weighted with a bit of modelling clay. Hold it lightly so that the weight can swing freely on about 10 inches/15 cm of thread. You can use either hand, and witches often find that if they are right-handed, their left is more sensitive for dowsing. Get the pendulum to identify 'Yes' and 'No' by holding it over your other hand held open. Say, 'Show me Yes,' and see what happens. If you concentrate you will see that the bob is starting to swing, either in a straight line or in a circle. If it hardly moves, ask it to show you more clearly.

It will move if you relax and let the bob swing. When you can see what it is doing for 'Yes', ask for a 'No'. This will be different, either a straight or circular swing in the opposite direction, or if it swung in a circle for 'Yes' it might do a straight line for 'No'. So long as these are clear and different you can go on to other uses. One will be testing plants or lists of cures for illness, as well as being used over a sick friend to try to locate the cause of discomfort.

Being able to dowse with a pendulum is one of the oldest and most useful Crafts, and well worth experimenting with until you get quick and clear answers. Always test what is 'Yes' and 'No' on each occasion, for the pendulum's movements, coming from your subconscious mind, may vary for many reasons.

You can try to locate sacred sites on a map spread out on a flat surface. Hold the pendulum in your most sensitive hand and with one finger of the other hand, point to various woods, streams, springs, parks, farmlands, ancient standing stones and anything else that interests you, asking 'Could I try working magic here?' or 'Is this place connected with the traditional powers of the Earth?'. Then watch its reaction. When it gives a definite 'Yes' over a place add it to a list to go and explore. All the time keep the question, 'Can I worship my Gods here?', or 'Is this a place I might go to receive guidance with my magic?'. You will soon find a variety of locations to explore. Take the dog, or a child, perhaps, and wander about with all your psychic senses switched on full. Be prepared to be surprised.

An ideal spot might turn up, which feels right, is secluded yet nearby, which has trees, water, a hill or some other natural features which make it welcoming and magical. Read any book, fictional or factual, on shamanism, and all of them talk about 'power spots', 'finding your place', and so on. Go out and actually do it for yourself. That is what the Craft is about – being in contact with the Earth and the powers of Nature! You will begin to sense them or see them and can build up a friendship and partnership, if you act with honour.

Not only should you explore your immediate area, although this will certainly show up places for everyday rites and meditations, but you should also, by taking a larger map, sort out some really special places for major festivals or gatherings and get to know them also. Always ask the Great Ones to guide you and keep you safe and psychically secure and you will not be troubled. Master the ancient arts of meditation and inner journeying so that you can bring your power spots home for the night, revisiting them astrally when you are not able to go there in person. Meditation is not something that only Eastern magicians and Buddhists do, but it is a really useful technique, to bring calm and insights, inspiration direct from the Goddess and power to your workings, either alone or shared. Work at it, no matter what sort of pagan or witch you intend to become. If you can't do that, why should the Great Ones bother with you? You have to find their secret places, learn their magical language of symbolism, altered states of controlled awareness and meditational experiences.

If you are lucky enough to have a garden, you can dedicate it to your chosen deities. For example, all healing and culinary herbs are sacred to the Earth Mother, and all white-flowered and scented plants are dedicated to the Moon. All yellow or orange flowers, especially sun-shaped ones, are special to the Sun God, and most prickly plants represent his antlered Hunter/Hero aspect. Even the most innocent flowerbed can have secret messages spelled out by colour, shape and pattern, but the gods will recognize it. Add in other magical features, stones from sacred places (not bits of standing stones or the like, but beach pebbles or mountain rocks) sea shells, lumps of water-carved wood, bark or elegant branches stripped bare in the ocean and deposited on a beach. Use visits to your chosen sacred place to find such items which can become features in your 'nature garden' or wild flower path, or butterfly border. Grow some of the taller shrubs that will screen an area for quiet meditation; never mind the thundering juggernauts and overflying jumbos, if you can meditate, you won't even hear these!

Seek out things for yourself in places where they are seen as rubbish, rather than buying decorative items from a garden centre. Look out for those lovely terracotta heads of Gods and Goddesses that are designed for plants, and hang them on a sunny wall, filled with such herbs as lobelia or creeping thyme, adorning the Old Ones with growing green hair. No one would accuse you of witchcraft for having such features as these on your patio.

If you don't even have a tiny garden plot in which you can plant and design a sacred space then you will have to resort to an older pagan practice. That is 'Tree Worship' for which the Druids, those Oak Priests of old, were famous. They did not create shrines or temples, they discovered, by divination or oracular visions, a place which was already sacred. It might have been a spring of pure water, a healing rock, a magical tree or a Goddess-haunted cave. Today we would discover such places either by dowsing on a map, or by following ley lines or energy streams. (Dowsing is another of the thirteen traditional arts which witches have always mastered, hence a gathering of thirteen, one of each sort of expert.)

All through the history of the common folk, since the earliest times, these sacred natural places and objects have been the secret centres of worship, requests for healing, for making offerings. Each of them is natural, chosen as holy because it was holy already. It was made by the Creator, untouched by human shaping, unlike chapels or mosques which are built. Anyone with an ounce of awareness can locate a tree which is, by its position, energy or nature, holy. There you can sit and silently make your pleas, ask for calmness, offer the traditional gifts of water, a pin (which in earlier times was actually quite a valuable commodity), and a strip torn from your garment and tied in the branches. Various customs along these lines are still celebrated in some places, like 'Bawming the Thorn' (adorning the sacred thorn tree, a Goddess symbol, with ribbons in Cheshire in July). Flowers and ribbons and garlands are hung around an ancient thorn tree and children dance about it.

On your own you don't need to go to those lengths, although if the tree is in your garden you can decorate it, make offerings of water, fertilizer, compost and so on, as well as burying requests for help beneath it, if possible written on a leaf or piece of bark. Here you will find runes or oghams are easier than curved letters. You can tie single threads or various-coloured wools, chopped into short lengths so that birds can take them to line their nests, or simply make decorations of seeds, nuts and stale bread, which wild birds and small creatures can feast upon. These are good offerings in the winter. Even posies of seed heads, grasses and thistles will be enjoyed by some of the rarer garden birds, and will not spoil the tree.

Do make an effort to acknowledge the phases of the Moon and Sun by being out there in their light. Learn to be still, silent and inwardly focused so that you can detect the subtle energies which affect all our psychic lives. Watch your dreams when your own Gods and Goddesses will inspire you, and be willing to give thanks, in a natural way, for those blessings which come your way. Try to find ways of secretly sharing your magic with the world around you, not by indiscriminately interfering with the love lives, health or financial matters of those about you, but by finding the reasons behind the troubles which affect the whole planet. Find ways to help the local environmentalists preserve places of natural beauty, or make more of the countryside available for others to appreciate. Here you would be completely out of step to be marching around in robes and cloaks, although a comfortable green coat and a single wild flower in your buttonhole would link you gently with the forces of Nature.

If you have no garden, live in a city and can't easily get to a park, you might consider volunteering to join a conservation team. Almost everywhere has these projects where groups of people get together, either in the evenings and weekends or, on larger or overseas restoration works, for weeks at a time. Usually there are team leaders who are experts in tree conservation, river restoration or wild animal assistance who are desperate to find helpers, and whole families and even young children are encouraged to take part. You will find experts who know about the old crafts of coppicing hazel, or using other wood for timber, or making besoms or hurdles or all kinds of things. Usually everyone on these schemes has a love for Nature, even if they aren't all setting out to become village witches, and can help you identify trees or plants and learn about their uses. Not only will you be sharing with like-minded people but you will be healing some of the neglect or destruction that people have wrought on Nature.

You will learn valuable skills, make friends and perform tasks which will bring pleasure to anyone who can then walk in those woods, sail on that canal, or simply watch birds and animals in an enriched and safer habitat. You may get wet and muddy, and have to stay in simple accommodation, but these schemes are run all over the world, so that participation in a local project can put you in touch with others working in Africa, India or the rainforests of the Amazon. Some schemes are on a very small scale, for example, helping an old peoples' home set up a herb garden, or making a shady garden for schoolchildren to enjoy. Even taking an old or unwell person's dog for a walk can help you get in touch with wilder and more natural places if you are scared to go there alone.

Of course, you need to be careful not to expose yourself to danger from, for example, unpleasant people, deep water, or high cliff edges. There are a great number of footpaths shown on walkers' maps which wander well clear of roads and traffic and safely cross some of the most beautiful and unspoiled landscapes. Even exploring towns and cities can produce some fascinating discoveries, like Green Men decorations on Victorian houses, hidden corners of history, wells and springs which still gush clear water in urban streets, or old graveyards where the bones of our ancestors lie after hundreds of years in grassy plots, at the feet of ancient yews.

Remember, underneath every street and city lie the bones of Mother Earth, and towns often have more varieties of plants, wild birds and even open spaces where people are free to roam than great tracts of monoculture farmlands. By caring for a garden, learning the names and uses of trees and plants, feeding wild creatures, erecting nesting boxes for birds, or simply observing the sky at night, when most of the world sleeps, you are closer to the lives of the old witches than you might be otherwise. Witchcraft is a spiritual partnership with Nature, and an understanding of the tides and seasons, the gifts and exchanges between the wilderness and the lives of mankind, is essential. Some people live by taking from Mother Nature, demanding attention from the elemental beings or the old deities, expecting them to appear at the wave of an athame, commanding them to appear or depart to suit their ritual needs. No one should treat their friends like that, and they should not order the forces of Creation around either.

Seven

RELIGION AND THE PAGAN PATH

I am a pagan. The Earth is my Mother,

and the Heavens my Father.

My religion is the adoration of life.

All Living things are part of my family.

I have walked this Earth before,

and be very sure, at this life's end,

I shall return.

Dan Hussey

One of the things which attracts people to witchcraft or, more likely, wicca, is the idea of a different religion. But the beliefs of today's pagans are very hard to pin down. It is said that if you have five pagans in a room and ask their opinion on their faith you will get at least seven answers. Most traditional religions have developed within a people or area through an appearance of a god or goddess in a particular place, who gives instructions to a priesthood, which in turn passes the tenets of the religion on to the people. More recent monotheist religions have developed around a book, be it the Bible, the Koran or the Torah. In each case a revelation has been given to a prophet who wrote down his god's words, and presented them to those who were to follow that faith. In earlier pagan practices there were often several goddesses and gods who actually appeared to the people, probably in places already considered sacred, like springs or by magical rocks, and brought blessings. The religions of books offer one male god, who doesn't even have a proper name, and doesn't show himself so followers have no idea what he looks like. It is expressly forbidden in many such Books of Rules to make idols or even likenesses of God the Father, or even his prophets. In earlier times the temples of the pagan deities were filled with the most glorious works of art honouring their many patron gods and goddesses.

When the written word replaced the apparition of the gods the first idea to be eliminated was the idea of a female god, a Great Mother or the many goddesses who people the oldest faiths. The new God of the Bible was a lone parent, a male god who brought forth creation from himself, and his follow-ers had no mother to look to for guidance or help. When he created the first man, Adam, he was born from dust or clay and he was alone. In some ver-sions of the creation myth, only later was a mate, called Eve, made from his rib. There are older stories of Adam first being helped by a female goddess, Lilith, who had the feet of an owl and wings, but she refused to submit to Adam's desires and fled. God sent three angels to fetch her back but she wouldn't go, so he was forced to create Eve. Even that story has been changed to weaken woman's power, by saying she led Adam to disobey God by eating the fruit of the Tree of Knowledge of Good and Evil. She wanted knowledge, God wanted a submissive wife to his first man, so they were both driven out of paradise, which is actually a walled garden. The rest is history, as they say, or perhaps myth.

In ancient Assyria, Chaldea and Egypt there were many goddesses and gods, each with particular specialities, or sacred centres. They were equal and free to live their own divine lives, assist their worshippers, offer oracles and instructions, heal the sick, bring victory in war, as well as caring for mothers in childbirth and their children. There were goddesses of war and wisdom, of protection and vengeance, as well as gentle maidens who cared for wild animals. Some gods taught the arts of healing, of music and poetry, or were rapists and liable to make love to any female being, human or otherwise. They had special festivals when processions to their temples were made by people carrying offerings of flowers, incense or animals for sacrifice. Sacred days were held when they were expected to appear, perhaps to their priests and priestesses inside the inner sanctum of their shrines, but their followers believed they were immanent.

Because the three great faiths of the West are monotheistic they have encouraged love and worship of male gods and their divine Sons or prophets, but they have not encouraged worship of the Mother, so women's position has often been seen as that of a possession rather than a free spirit. In some places attempts were made to reintroduce a sacred female figure. In Judaism there is the idea of the Shekinah, the Bride of God, in whose honour the Shabbat meal is prepared. In Roman Catholicism, the Virgin Mary, Mother of Christ, has prominence and festivals, as do many female saints. Some of these certainly have taken over from earlier pagan goddesses and nymphs who guarded sacred springs or groves, for example. Even in Islam, Fatima, the sister of Mohammed, is honoured in some sects. It is as if people, who, according to Dr Carl Jung, have an in-built impulse to worship, have been trying to allow a goddess figure to re-enter their religious observances. In the middle of the twentieth century this impulse took off in a new direction, and gave rise to wicca and its pagan religion which honours goddesses, in some cases, above their gods.

Although each individual modern pagan will have his or her own ideas of how and why they consider themselves pagans, a few basic tenets are shared by most of them. Because there is no one book of rules, no single primary sacred centre of pagan worship, no religious buildings, trained and accre- dited priesthoods or fixed festival dates, anyone can make their own religious practices. However, there are a few things that most pagans accept. One is that there is a great Goddess, and that she is equal to, or, in a few more extreme cases, superior to a god or several goddesses. Others believe that 'All gods are one god and all goddesses are one goddess and that there is one Initiator or Creator', to quote Dion Fortune, a very magical lady who died in 1946. There is a general belief in what is called, in sanskrit, 'Karma', which means that for every action there is an equal reaction, and that in life you are personally responsible for everything you do, for better or worse, and will have to rebalance any discrepancy later. Most modern pagans accept the idea of reincarnation, in that our human souls are immortal and will return to life many times, to experience and learn, and hopefully evolve towards the best we may be.

Wiccan groups, inspired by the books of Gerald Gardner, Doreen Valiente, Stewart and Janet Farrar, Starhawk, and many other early witchcraft writers in Britain and America, have established a set of usually eight ritual occasions throughout the year when their covens meet for a Sabbat. Wiccans also have initiations led by a High Priestess and a High Priest who admit newcomers after prior instruction, perhaps in an 'outer court' or training group. Each group is independent and, despite the fact that when covens have more than thirteen regular members they may hive-off daughter covens, there is no register of groups, or that much interaction between them or their members. In Britain, however, there are national Federations of Pagans which anyone can join, and so participate in conferences, open rituals and social gatherings, which can often be a first step towards finding a coven or other group. No one knows exactly how many witches, who often work their magic alone, or coven members there are world-wide these days, but most commentators agree that this particular version of paganism is spreading more rapidly than any other religious impulse at the start of the twenty-first century.

Because covens are small groups they usually meet in people's houses or out of doors in traditional sacred sites, in woods or by standing stones. Although there are a great many individual wiccans, because they aren't organized, they don't own any special places or temples in Britain where new-comers might go to find out more. In the USA there is much more structure, with family trees and relationships between covens, initiations and traditions, and some groups do own land, run centres and provide on-going training, conferences and gatherings. The idea behind the House Church is very much part of the way of the witches, who need somewhere to form their circles, celebrate their festivals and mark the full moons by their gatherings.

Individual or solo witches work alone, or with a few friends or family members, and they conduct their rites out of doors, in woods, fields, on river banks or by the sea, coming quietly and secretly to their chosen spot, per-forming their acts of magic, and vanishing into the countryside like mist. No one gives them permission, or objects to them, for they drift gently over the land, seldom even leaving footprints. This is very different to the unheeding

New Age worshipper who goes to sacred or ancient and protected sites, drips enduring candle wax on delicate lichens, digs holes in precious wildflower-filled turf and leaves rubbish and unspeakable offerings which will not decay and could kill wildlife as a memento of their visits.

For many of these wiccans and new pagans there does seem to be a need for direction, lists of rules or a Book of Shadows, leaders and instructors, regular meetings and initiations and degrees. These strictures give them stability and a feeling of 'belonging' to a religious society. All this after having rejected their previous faith because of its regulations, fixed festivals, distant priesthood, and so on. However, there are others who bravely recognize that witchcraft is a daring philosophy, and they have sought to make the links that count, not with an organized paganism, but directly with the forces of Nature herself. There are three things which many modern people appear to fear above anything else. These are stillness, silence and solitude, yet these are the very things which give a witch her or his power.

If you are absolutely still it allows those subtle senses to come into play, when you can reach beyond the limitations of your physical form to enter the other realities of magic. If you are silent you can allow your inner hearing to listen to the voices of the Earth Mother and the spirits of Nature, the wild birds and animals, which even in a city may be heard if you let them. If you are alone you will be able to pay attention to the beings of the unseen realms which surround us, whether you call them gods and goddesses, angels, elementals or devas. These are gifts of the lone witch, especially those individuals who dare to go to the wild and unspoiled places where the wilderness touches the hearts of towns. It is by deliberately distancing yourself from the clutter of modern life that you can reconnect to the forces of creation, healing and joy which are all waiting to be heard.

People so fear being alone that they have created endless modern toys to ward off this experience. Where can you go these days where people are not plugged into their electronic baubles? Every train or bus echoes to the discordant songs of the siren mobile phones, every home has its computer with e-mail, internet and games to prevent its owners from using their minds, their natural talents of inspiration, or from holding normal, face to face conversations. The phone chat is so inane, 'I'm in the bus/train/airport/car ...' What does it matter? For centuries people first communicated by speaking to each other, then they could write letters which took time to arrive, then the telephone allowed conversations across distances, and now all the electronic messaging adds another dimension through which worthless chatter can prevent us from hearing ourselves think. If you want to be a pagan you will have to relearn the old arts of self-reliance, talking in person, awaiting an answer, really listening and replying. You can't e-mail the gods, though I am sure some people will try.

True religion is about making a direct, personal and individual communication with unseen beings, being freely able to ask questions, to receive guidance, healing and practical help. It is knowing that you are celebrating a particular festival because it is meaningful to you and your friends. It is understanding the words of prayers, invocations and spells because you have chosen them, not because you have read them, or been told them by a priest. It is being able to debate among your companions how best to symbolize an element, or discover by direct inner revelation the next step on your own magical path. Organized faiths, including many branches of contemporary paganism, have rules and ritual dates, they have books of instruction, they have bodies of information which must not be altered or questioned, but received as holy writ, even though they were constructed by poets in the 1950s. Perhaps that is what you, as an individual, want, and you may crave a community where you can participate in festivals, initiations, have rituals spelled out for you and have a priest/priesteshood to look up to. However, there is a far more daring alternative.

This is the path of the old country witch, which seeks the powers of Nature in nature, which takes the dates of feasts from what the land and its goddess is actually offering. If the hawthorn is in bloom then you can celebrate the Coming of May, if the corn harvest has been cut you can acknowledge the corn spirit in the last sheaf, if the first delicate white and green spears of the 'snow piercers' are above the dark earth of winter, you can welcome 'Bride' at Candlemas. How can you have a nature religion if the very forces of Nature which give us life, food, homes and indirectly most of the things we use, are completely ignored because some writer has said Lammas is 1 August? A spiritual path which is linked to the seasons, the land and the growing of plants has to accept, especially in these strange times, when the weather conditions are out of line due to global warming, that Nature still matters. If we paid more heed to what the Earth Mother is actually doing, and less to what we are told or are being led to accept, humanity wouldn't have done as much damage to the world as we have.

Although many of today's witches are pagans, there is no historical evidence that their predecessors were anything but followers of the religion of their time and place. Today people are freer to believe what they will, worship what gods and goddesses they choose, in any way and at any festivals they like. It is worth understanding what brought about this quiet religious revolution which has sprung from Britain in the twentieth century. Modern witches like to participate in rituals, seasonal celebrations and magical and pagan gatherings of many kinds. To try to understand what has led to these developments it is also necessary to look at the importance of legends, traditional happenings, old customs and ancient, sacred places to modern pagans.

Witchcraft is as old as the hills, this is well known, but are its adherents in the twenty-first century really practising a religion with an unbroken tradition of 5,000 years or more? Did the thousands of people who suffered and died in the middle ages really adhere to an ancient pagan faith, worshipping a Horned God and a Moon Goddess? Did they die for their beliefs or were they victims of a biased god-fearing clergy and the political toils of their time which used them as scapegoats for its own bigotry? Probably the most honest and exact answer is, 'No one knows.' If there were pagan traditions kept alive in calendar customs, or in village celebrations or in the hearts of pagans through the ages, they have left no traces that any historian, social researcher or even witch can identify as valid. There is little actual evidence that any of the people tried and executed for witchcraft and sorcery were actually what we would recognize as witches, but all were *victims*.

Whatever these unfortunate people were thought to have been doing it didn't include worshipping a goddess, meeting in magical circles, performing seasonal celebrations or being led by a High Priestess or High Priest, as modern covens are now. Some were supposed to have put spells on people, or caused their cattle to die, or their milk to go sour. Some were accused of ill wishing, having the 'evil eye' or being able to turn into animals or fly through the air. If these were the ancestors of modern witches, how many of these arts are still possible? Were they possible five or six hundred years ago? It is true that the power to heal is the flip side of the coin to the power to curse. Both these ancient arts draw on the ability to manipulate the life force, preferably to benefit someone. Anyone with a practical knowledge of herbs and plant remedies will certainly be able to recognize the deadly ones, and know how to prepare them, just as they would the healing herbs.

In the modern world we have science to explain theories of disease, that illness is usually caused by bacteria or viruses, that different conditions have different causes, and are caught in a variety of ways. Scientists have devised effective cures for many serious diseases, and some have been eradicated from the world through treatment and vaccination. What medical science hasn't fully explained is that the agents which cause many illnesses are all around us, all the time. Every breath we take is filled with minute disease-causing microbes, yet we do not fall ill every day. Something extra has to make us vulnerable. In the old days it was sometimes thought that sickness came about through dark magic or ill-wishing by an annoyed neighbour, but today no one even considers this. Most of us are glad we are in reasonable health and give little heed to what makes us sick, or prevents us from catching flu when everyone else has it. We don't usually attribute this to magic or to the whim of the gods. It just is.

Because people didn't understand what made animals ill or caused fields of crops to be struck by some infection or other, they looked for scapegoats to blame these natural misfortunes on. Often the chosen victim was a woman who might have begged for food and upset those around her in some other way. Remember, there were no pensions for old widows, and women, even in the middle ages, often outlived their menfolk, who might also have gone off to war and not returned. There was little help for the old, the sick or the disliked. Originally, in pre-Christian times, the people had turned to the temples for healing or for explanations of droughts or strange happenings. The priests often offered healing, or the priestesses called forth oracles to explain these mysteries of life, but the Christian church was afraid of magic, and though it acknowledged the miracle of transsubstantiation, healing and dealing with the future were outside its remit. What it feared it attacked.

It is true that there have been, for all time, people more learned in the use of magic to bring success to the hunt, more aware of the effects of herbs for healing in sickness – but these are crafts, a skill natural or encouraged, but not the application of religion or worship. Witches wielded no authority within their communities, but were people whose help was sought to deal with life's misfortunes. They never wanted fame or power or glory, but, like any other skilled worker, they used their talents for the benefit of those around them. Some people do seem to inherit psychic skills even today, just as they do musical perfect pitch, or the ability to run fast. The qualities of the mind are just as genetic as qualities of the body, and the circumstances in which children grow up influence them just as much as their genetic make up. If a child is allowed to hear music from an early age, or taste fine food, or play sport, he or she will grow up retaining these appreciations. If witches taught their children how to sing the spells, how to recognize the healing herbs, how to communicate with animals, then they would grow up with more access to these abilities, hundreds of years ago or today. These magical arts and crafts need not be aspects of a religion, pagan or otherwise.

Although various people have claimed, or it has been claimed for them, that so-and-so is King or Queen of the Witches, the very nature of the Craft forbids anyone taking such a title. In the past, witches often came from the lower walks of life, and though skilled and knowledgeable in their own field, they were, and still are, basically humble people. There is no point in publicizing oneself with grandiose titles, for those who know can see through the phony facade to the individual inside, and through the person too. Anyone with real knowledge of the Craft does not seek recognition – he or she knows that witches will know their own. Those who seek truly will find a genuine teacher. As to the idea that witches are only made by initiation, the mind boggles. It may happen, though, that initiation will bring out hidden abilities and open doors to the unconscious that were apparently firmly closed.

Esoteric power cannot be bought and sold or even given away like a material object. It is a seed that sleeps within mankind and it may awaken to life in many different ways. Death does not destroy it and, once it has begun to grow, the soul of that person is enhanced in many ways. The initiate of one life does not necessarily need a further initiation in each subsequent life, nor can a ceremony alone bring to life the seed of inherited witch power, especially where the candidate is unknown to his future coven at the time of admittance. It has long been a tradition of the Craft that one is reborn among one's previous friends and family, and this is perhaps the greatest test of survival of the Craft. To know and be known already by those around you can be a very great experience.

As to the worship of the Gods, this is not as dogmatic as some writers would lead one to believe. If the ritual and dogma, allegedly passed down intact from time immemorial, are adhered to so rigorously that the spark of life they contained is crushed to extinction, these 'witches' are doing just what the Christians (whom many witches seem to abhor) have done, and the hypocrisies will arise in the same way. These people are not following the Old Religion but attempting to nurture a dead one. To believe so rigidly in a Horned God and Moon Goddess may be a religion to some (and the idea that people have worshipped these forms of deities for ages may give them support) – but religion is not belief, it is knowledge and personal experience of the Gods, not supplications to a cardboard replica as laid down by some other person.

Anyone who has worked magic, whether as a witch or High Magician, knows that there is a power greater than humankind, and may at some time experience it manifesting in different ways, perhaps as one aspect of the Moon Goddess, or as the Sun God, but these are real rather than hallucinations or visions. In the same way, a witch working in abstract terms brings about changes in you and your surroundings so that what you encounter is not a fantasy but something absolutely real. To call upon the power of the Old Gods from the Time Without Words is to invoke the power of the tempest and the wrath of the storm. It is the destroying flash of lightning, and this does not heal, nor restore the lost, nor foretell the future: yet these are the gods of the Oldest Religion.

In prehistoric times, healing was the kind deity who led the sick gently through the gates of death to the quiet pain-free place where they would wait to be reborn whole and full of life. Divination, then, was knowing where the herds of food animals were to be found in the time of hunger. Now, we don't need a crystal ball to find a supermarket!

This might horrify some witches – perhaps you know and perceive life and the gods in a different way which you are certain is right for you. Let it be so. If you can look with clear eyes into your own open heart and say, 'I live as I worship and there is no deed of my hand or my mind or my heart which is not worthy of my Gods', then all is well. It is right to live in worship, for the

Gods are in all things and any act which is cruel or causes harm is an insult to them. Does each day bring exultation within your heart with the morning, and peace and tranquillity with the evening – or does the pace of modern life leave you no time to appreciate living, and to feel the touch of the hands of the Goddess? Perhaps you are a 'weekend witch' and the book rites give you satisfaction – if you become a 'whole-life witch' you will find this satisfaction develops a thousand fold.

Many of you will have trodden a lonely path, finding healing in the feel of the earth and air and in the scent of flowers. You will have received the blessing of the trees, and the power of the changing seasons take their proper place in your life. You will have drunk the bitter wine of the cauldron and eaten the harsh bread of experience, well-seasoned with the salt of fortune. The cords unify, they do not punish, and the plough joins those inside the circle. The Great Ones come freely to keep you company, your prayers request not compel. You know the mysteries of the open flower, and the place that is between the worlds. To you, and those who are yet to come to learn these things, be aware that you will have to discover beliefs for yourself, rather than accepting what others say. You will have to learn ancient arts which, because they work in secret, are hard to understand, but if you take them as real, they will become effective. You will have to take responsibility for your actions, because you will know that thoughts are things and that every move you make can affect the rest of the world.

Like all beliefs, modern paganism has its own tenets and ideals, but the greatest difference between paganism and Christianity, for example, is that the Christians are taught to believe, the pagans come to know the deities they worship. This simple concept makes a world of difference, for the pagan aims to establish a two-way contact with the Gods, whereas more conventional beliefs require continuous worship from the believer. Pagans also accept the idea of reincarnation and this gives them a far wider view of human life and activities.

A witch who knows she or he will return to earth should have a rather different attitude to another who accepts the idea of 'three score years and ten' being his full share of living. In each incarnation a person acquires karma, or rather is subject to its laws, in that if you cause harm to another person, or are linked through love, there will be an opportunity in another life to repay or to complete a relationship from the past. By helping others and seeking to advance on the spiral of evolution your burden will be lessened until your purpose of earthly incarnations has been achieved. A great deal could be written about a pagan's quest to come into direct and personal contact with the forms of the Goddess he or she prays to or the God she or he calls upon for aid. This is a personal quest and will certainly lead to individual experiences which have no match in other fields of life, nor can they be truly explained in words.

We have probably become too civilized to speak as freely with the gods as did our forebears, for we in the West have created our own environment and lost touch with nature. Today few of us, in our offices, or factories, or in the supermarkets, are aware of the state of the tide, the direction of the wind, or even the state of the weather, for much of the time. Why should we be? It doesn't matter to us now. We have become cut off from the Earth Mother and by forgetting her ways we are now separated from our natural heritage, and that loss is sorely felt, if not recognized. This is a double loss for, by ignoring the tides of nature, we often unknowingly work against them, causing ourselves trouble and hardship. Through forgetting Mother Nature we are cruel to her, destroying her plants and wildlife, polluting her rivers, spoiling the very air we need to breathe, through greed or expediency, or more often sheer ignorance. We owe her a great debt and it is unlikely we can ever repay it.

To try to re-establish the balance is indeed a great task and, though pagan at heart, you may say to yourself, 'What can I do? I am helpless against all the harm that has already been done.' There is a great deal that everyone can do, especially if you wish to return to the arms of Mother Nature and receive her forgiveness. Most of the things are unpleasant, like clearing up rubbish you may find at some beauty spot, choosing some local ancient site and trying to see that litter is not allowed to accumulate. If you look upon these places as temples of Mother Nature, then care and attention given to them is service to her. If you can teach your children respect for the countryside, allowing them to cherish rather than destroy the wild flowers, they will grow up with the idea that such places are sacred. Few folk would deliberately drop rubbish in a church or museum – why should they be allowed to do so in the holy places of the Old Ones?

When you gather the fruits of Nature's wild harvest be sure to leave some fruit or flowers behind so that next year there will be another chance to gather her bounty. Try not to break bushes or plants when you pluck from them. Don't damage growing crops or frighten cattle or sheep when crossing farmland. There are a great number of wild ways free to be walked and enjoyed, and a little care and forethought can prevent such places being spoiled or put 'out of bounds' for others. In Britain, excellent ramblers' maps may be used, showing marked footpaths, viewpoints, ruins, ancient monuments, springs, copses, field names and much more, indicating the rich heritage of Nature available to all. In the USA, 'Trails Illustrated' maps from the National Geographic Society or the large-scale area maps from the 'Geological Survey of the Unites States' show trails, old features and viewpoints, parks and so on in detail.

Many people are prepared to pick herbs or flowers, or gather foliage to use as Christmas decorations, but are slow to give thanks for this freely-given bounty. Many novice witches feel safe in calling upon the Goddess of Nature within the safety of their own homes, but few seem to have the determination to go out and call upon the Lord of the Wild Hunt, or the Earth Mother in her own place. Some feel that it is only possible to call upon the Great Ones if you know their particular names, or by using a well-tried ritual gleaned from some book. Some people fear to call upon the Gods in case something actually happens!

The Gods are all around us, all the time, wherever anything grows, be it a straggling pot plant on the office window ledge, or a forest scarcely touched by mankind in hundreds of years. Those that formed creation dwell within it, seen in the sky, felt in the touch of a soft breeze, experienced as a bitter storm or swirling snow. The rulers of the elements are all around us, whenever we step beneath their sky, and walk on their stones. This is the whole point of witchcraft, it is not a matter of theory, or of virtual experience, it is getting out there into the elements, on the bare earth, by moving water, or under the shade of great trees. Thinking, reading, using electronic knowledge are no substitutes for being there, and feeling, understanding and sensing to the fullest.

How, then, are you to get in touch with the Goddess, for example? What do you call her, how can you become aware of her presence? These, and many others, are the questions which novices often ask. Like most of real witchcraft, the answers are very simple, if you can find places which are natural to the Spirit of Nature – even in the cities there must be quiet spots where some part of the Great Ones may be encountered if your mind is receptive and still. Wait and let your thoughts drift away until you are ready to become aware of the Goddess near you. Ask within your heart that you may know she is with you. If it is the Lord of Life you seek, find a place in the sun and as his heat touches you ask to know him and understand his power. If at first results aren't very forthcoming try again. A pagan with no patience has missed the point of his faith. When conditions are right you will be aware of the Great presences, and you will know and not have to believe.

If you want to address the Goddess by name, you have an enormous choice. There are encyclopaedias of Goddesses which will give you some idea of the vastness of this study! The simplest, and often the best, forms of address are Lady, Goddess of ..., or Mother, depending on what aspect you wish to perceive. If that is too simple there is Flora, the Goddess of Flowers (that name is far easier to say than the Welsh Blodeuwedd, a lady created of blossoms). There is Mother Nature or Mother Cary, whose charges are all kinds of birds; even the bees, those 'smallest of fowl', are her children. In Somerset the river Cary outlines the figure of Virgo, the very pregnant maiden of the Earth zodiac, twelve miles across, who offers the sheaf of corn to the Sun King. On her fat belly is the village of Babcary, reputed to be 'easy to get into, but hard to get out'. Mother Cary is also Ceres, the Grain Goddess after whom cereals are named.

If you want to explore and develop a relationship with the Moon Goddess she may be simply called Luna, or have three names to fit her triple phases. She may also be encountered as the Egyptian goddess, Isis, with a green gown as Goddess of Earth, or crowned with the Horned Moon as the Goddess of Night. She is also Hathor, with cow's horns, Goddess of all beasts and children. The Greek myths and those of ancient Egypt, and of the western Celtic lands, give us many special names, and she will answer to any of them if they are called with love. Here you can use book knowledge to discover the myths and stories, the symbols, sacred days, the offerings, which, even now, are a valid part of this old worship, be they flowers or special incenses. Just reading other people's words or prayers will have no reality unless you enact them for yourself.

If you can still your racing thoughts, create an image in your mind's eye and then watch, you will certainly see what you seek. Some people feel they can only worship the Goddess within a specially set-up circle, when they have performed a ceremony to seal the place, not realizing that the Great Ones are in all things, and it is inner peace and quiet that is needful. A magic circle may well help you to alter your state of perception and so make you more aware, but the Goddess does not need to be called, merely seen. After all, if you have become as one of her children, through study, or initiation, or by that inner sense of belonging, you don't need a circle. When you wish to speak to your earthly friends and parents you don't need a special set-up, you just ring them, or visit them. It is the same with your Heavenly family. Give thanks, treat them with honour and the Great Ones will dwell in your heart and bless you. ⌒●

Once you have come to understand there is a living channel through which your desires can be sent to the Earth Mother or her consort, and that in return for honour and respect you will receive magical power, insights and guidance, a two-way communication will endure. You can start to understand why a circle of sacred dates might be needed, and know what each represents to you, both in your heart and in your life. These will not be meaningless repetitions of other folks' prayers, or mindless actions because it says so in some book, but a genuine, meaningful and uplifting experience you have gained for yourself.

Although most of the information in this book is aimed at individuals, it is perfectly reasonable to discover a community of like-minded people to share your country walks, develop meditations, cast sacred circles, sing spells, talk to the old gods and make magic together. Much of the practical work is made far easier when it is shared with companions: learning the names, uses and preparations of plant materials, for example, is so much easier if you can find an expert to teach you, although you can learn alone from books as you examine each living herb or tree. Once you feel ready, it can be fun to organize a picnic and celebration of harvest, or a simple ceremony for midwinter which you can share with open-minded family and friends. You don't have to declare that you are a pagan witch unless you want to. There are still many people who fear magic, witchcraft and occult skills of any sort, and their ignorance makes them attack anyone who holds such different views. The spread of information is alleviating some of this problem, but it hasn't entirely gone away.

To 'become a pagan' requires nothing of you, and you can freely declare yourself as a pagan to your friends, but if there are occasions when you have to put your religion on official forms, will you still write 'pagan'? If someone asks about your beliefs, will you have sensible and well-thought-out answers? Now is the time to start examining what you really believe, consider who told you, and what it means to your heart and soul. If you are rejecting a previous orthodox faith consider why? Why now? What is it you reject or dislike? Does your alternative religion meet your expectations? Have you encountered the Great Earth Mother or the Lord of the Sky or are these just phrases you could use to shock or upset your friends? Religion is for life, not just for Yuletide!

An exercise you can try might help you sort out your feelings. Ideally, this should be performed out of doors, in a natural place, and requires only that you act sincerely and with all your heart and abilities. Go to your chosen spot and carefully prepare a seat for the Earth Mother and her Lord, deck it with natural flowers or greenery, or lay pretty pebbles to form a ring. You may use a magical circle if you feel it is necessary and know how to set one up, but as you are trying to meet your divine ancestors, it isn't essential. Imagine you are about to greet an honoured and much loved guest, so prepare as well as you can, in any way which does not harm the place, or leave residues which will endure. Sit down opposite the place you have prepared for your holy visitor and make yourself calm and still.

Open your heart, your mind and all your senses to welcoming the Great Lady or Lord of the Wild. Speak to them in silence or aloud, depending where you are, and ask them to come gently to you, to meet and communicate. Stay still and quiet for as long as you can. About half an hour is the minimum, because it may take a while for your invitation to reach out to them. Listen for any sounds of their approach – even the calls of birds or the wind in the trees could be a message, for the Great Ones do not appear just how we want them to, when we ask. They come in their own way, and only by applying silence, stillness and often solitude, will you discover their presence. If you are lucky, they will make themselves known to you, in vision, sound or touch, so be prepared to be surprised. If you don't get immediate visions, speech or insights, try again, but always say thank you, and acknowledge that they may have come but you are not yet on the right wavelength to receive their visit. Make sure you clear up completely, as this is a good way of ensuring you have fully returned to everyday consciousness, and it also honours your working place. If you treat the land with respect you will always be welcomed.

Eight

THE ARTS OF RITUAL

There is a single main definition of the object of all magical Ritual.

It is the uniting of the Microcosm with the Macrocosm. The Supreme

and Complete Ritual is therefore the Invocation of the Holy Guardian

Angel, or in the language of Mysticism, Union with the Creator ...

Aleister Crowley, 'The Principles of Ritual', *Magic in Theory and Practice*

Many modern witches like to use rituals for their festivals, for initiations, for giving degrees and at full moons. Because covens usually have between five and thirteen members this sharing of activities binds the group together under the guidance of its High Priestess and High Priest. There is no evidence that such people organized celebrations or ceremonies in the past, however, and even today, many witches prefer to carry out their Craft alone or with a few companions. This does not prevent them using a variety of rituals though. Often these are designed on a one-off basis rather than being part of a repeated pattern as the yearly cycle turns. Also, individual witches are more inclined to use ritual as adjunct to their magic, to bless a talisman or charm, to empower a healing potion, to divine the future or to seek communion with the Earth Mother and her Lord of the Sky. It doesn't really matter if there is only one person performing a ritual, so long as every witch understands what they are aiming to achieve, and how the working is intended to bring about their intention. Intent, concentration and understanding the principles are what makes magic successful.

Every ritual, like a good book, has a plot or reason for being written; it has a beginning, a middle and an end, all of which relate to each other. Most witchcraft rituals, whether they are for a seasonal celebration or a personal healing spell require the demarcation of a sacred circle, the acknowledgment of the four directions or quarters, welcoming the powers most likely to assist in the operation and a closing segment. This often involves all present, both seen and unseen, sharing a ritual chalice of wine or fruit juice and eating some sacred bread or cake. This is all part of a very ancient love feast called, in Greek, the Agape, and does not intend to copy the Christian mass, which it predates by centuries. Some rituals are long, slow and wordy, with beautiful poetry and stately dances, others are short and sweet, simply being focused on making a magical space, developing a calm atmosphere and then consulting an oracle. Rituals should always end with some kind of thanksgiving, even if the participants aren't yet psychic enough to sense the presence of deities or powers of Nature around them.

Often what is most important in any ritual is the actual reason for doing it. In order to prepare, whether you are alone or sharing your work with others, it is essential to establish a main objective so that everyone involved can focus their attention on achieving that aim. As you become more expert at ritual you will find it is possible to dispense with some of the equipment, in fact those with sufficient practice can work entirely in their heads. For beginners, though, it does help to have a few basic symbolic objects to help set out your ritual space, mark the directions and signify the festival with flowers or a decorated altar. You will need to realize that as you begin to formulate your aim and purpose for any ritual you are actually beginning to work on it. For this reason it is important to be very clear and precise as to what you are intending to do. This is especially true if there are several of you, and one contingent imagines you are celebrating Lammas and the rest think it will be a healing rite. That would lead to being at cross purposes and wasting valuable energy and direction. Agree absolutely first on a single aim, and write it down, whether it is for making a simple talisman, singing a spell or doing a tarot reading. Later you can check how well you did.

Once you have decided on the objective you will need to make decisions about how complicated or simple you will make the working, whether you will have lots of words, and if so where they are to be spoken from. If you prefer the old outdoor form of witchcraft, where spoken or sung words were quite a small part of the ritual, with symbolic actions indicating to the old gods what was required, then you will have to devise suitable ways of enacting your request. Although you will have read books which show all sorts of knives, statues, cords, candles and other impedimenta as being vital to witchcraft, this is not necessarily the case. If you are outside you can see the Earth, our Great Mother, you may be able to see the Moon, her daughter, or the Sun, her lover, so why should you need an image? You don't have to wave a knife at your own dearest family and divine ancestors. Why would you want to scourge your friends who have done you no harm, or bind them with cords if they are working with you? Suffering is not an effective teacher; most people learn valuable lessons by watching someone who is an expert performing that task, and then being gently encouraged to try it for themselves. A lot of what has been written about the essentials for witch magic is simply not true. You must consider every action or text and make up your own mind.

You may need four simple and ordinary things to place at the edges of your circle, and these can be a common pebble for earth, a small bowl or even a seashell of water, a real flame on a candle or lantern for fire, though a gold, red or orange flower would do, and either a joss stick, or scented flower, bird's feather or fan for air. In the centre you stand yourself, the container of the elements, plus a divine spark of the creative force, as you are alive. If you intend to share a communion with your companions, or just with the Great Ones, you will need a goblet of wine and a piece of bread or cake. You will need matches to light the incense and candle, and a bottle opener possibly for the wine, but the whole collection of these items will fit into a small bag.

Real witchcraft requires items made with your own hands, to your own designs, to the best of your ability, in honour of your deities. It might take you a while to locate a suitable tree from which you can cut a branch for a wand, or discover a seashell on the beach, or find a stone which pleases you with its colour and has a nice feel, but patience is a virtue for everyone, and essential to every witch. Learning to recognize a hazel when you see one is an early step, knowing when the tide will be ebbing so that you can walk on the shore, or where you might locate a suitable pebble comes from seeking with the heart. Performing rituals involves knowing that you have all the simple equipment, and that you have an objective that only a magical ritual will fulfil.

Each time you work your witchcrafts you will need to begin by connecting yourself to the earth beneath your feet and the sky above, to the Mother of Nature, and the Lord of Life. It may help you to stand upright, with bare feet on the ground, and imagine that you are like a tree, rooted strongly into the land from which you draw spiritual nourishment. Pause and sense your own stability and strength. Consider the bones of your hips forming a kind of bowl, a symbol within you of water. If you are a woman, consider your womb, the watery place which nurtures a child before its own independent life. In your heart is the place of the fire of love and passion, of caring and concern, of sympathy and joy, where a flame of life burns throughout your being. Above that, in your throat is the passage of air, which gives you the power of speech, to communicate with humans, spirits of the wild and with the great gods, in song and spell, in incantation and enchantment. In your head is the power of the divine, the spiritual flame of magical power, given to all who seek it, from the source of light above. It is the seat of second sight, clairvoyance and intuition where your witch powers may be located within the focused mind. Remember, you are all elements, all powers, and a channel for the pure light of good within the earth, if you use your magic effectively.

To begin to create a sacred space, clear a circle: out of doors you may sweep it with the witches besom, marking out a ring large enough for your purpose. There is no fixed size. Be sure you know where the directions are, so that you can start by walking to the northern edge of the circle, the place of earth and the creative darkness of midnight. See beyond you, clearly in your mind's eye, a great dark forest, sleeping under the stars, clothing the sides of a great mountain, which is the body of the Earth Mother. Sing to her, asking for strength and endurance, patience and common sense in your ritual. Take as long as you need for the feelings, images and sensations to become real. It may not work at first, but gradually your inner vision will get better and the Mountain of the Mother will appear before you.

Next go to the eastern point of your circle, and see the sky lighten before sunrise, with the midnight blue of night fading with the coming dawn. Perceive the wind brushing your cheek like the touch of your beloved, and fields of grain rippling in the morning breeze filling the whole of your vision. Smell the scents of flowers, woodsmoke and incense, drifting towards you and awakening your inner senses. Sing a song of dawning and the commencement of magic, which recalls the dawn chorus of the birds, and the first breath of a young child. Ask for inspiration and enlightenment in all that you do.

Go to the southern edge of your circle, and think of the blazing heat of noon, when the sky is white and the sun burns down, driving away the shadows of doubt. See the outline of a great volcano, spewing hot, red rivulets of lava, or a huge bonfire, blazing and sparking on a barren, rocky landscape. Acknowledge the power of the Lord of Flame, called Bran or Lleu or Ra, and sing a powerful song that calls for courage, determination, the ability to choose, and the energy to accomplish what you want to achieve without fear.

Now go to the West, and imagine you stand on the edge of the ocean whose ever-moving waters wash your feet. Here is the dimming at twilight as the sun sets into the scarlet horizon, and the blue and green and grey of the water reflects into the darkening sky. Feel a sense of purification at the touch of the waves, and the suck and roar of the sea bringing a deep calmness and repose to your soul. Sing a gentle lullaby that asks for cleansing of body, mind and spirit, that will wash away the tensions and troubles of the everyday world, into the great ocean of peace. Ask for the ability to truly understand your own motives, and those of other people, and the wisdom to find ways to bring peace to your life.

Then go to the centre of your ring and look up to the heavens where the starry wisdom flows down into earth, and look down where the rich earth provides nourishment for all that grows, and give out a song which joins all these ideas together in your own life and work. Be still for a while, then going to the northern edge of the circle again, begin to walk round, building a circle and then a globe of shining silvery light, which will protect and empower your working. Walk round slowly, clockwise, three times, feeling this sphere building around you. When you have completed this to your own satisfaction you may then get on to the main part of the ritual.

This is a way of calling the attention of the invisible realms of nature spirits, elemental beings and the Great Mother and Father of Earth to the fact that you need their help and awareness in the space of time to come. The clearer you are in your visualization the stronger the link will be, and the greater power you will be able to call upon. Of course if there are several of you, each can take a quarter, and you can elaborate this mental exercise into a physical one, by placing your symbols of the elements at each point of the compass, lighting a lantern, burning incense, or calling upon the names of a set of gods and goddesses from *one* single tradition, if you really know who they are. It is not safe to mix the names of deities from different lands or historical times, as they don't all get on with each other and you can end up with a disturbed muddle. It is far safer to use titles, like Lady of the Northern Lands, Lord of the Southern Skies and so on, as you will get precisely who you ask for and no one else.

Within the circle you can sit and perform a divination with cards or scry in a black mirror, if you have that skill. You can celebrate a festival, offering appropriate flowers and symbols of the season, you may work with the Moon, using her waxing and waning phases to empower a spell to increase or decrease something, depending on the moment and nature of the help needed. When you have completed your work, be silent for a few moments, then, starting with West, give a short prayer of thanks, moving on to the South, East and North, and finally the Centre. Take all your elemental symbols home with you. There are no fixed ways of doing any of these things for witches value spontaneity, and simple words spoken from the heart will be far more powerful than lengthy verses read from a book.

It will depend a lot upon where you live in the world as to how and when you celebrate the passing cycle of sacred festivals. You will need to learn when your first flowers of the year open, when the first butterfly will be seen, when winter begins, and at what time each important harvest from land or sea or orchard is to be gathered. This cycle of activity is real, and though many old activities have been changed by modern methods, underlying these, especially in the wilder places, even within cities, the ancient markers of time may be encountered if you bother to look for them. If you are sharing this voyage of self-awareness, magic and witchcrafts with some friends you will need to agree what marks each spoke of the annual wheel, even how many spokes you can recognize in your home region. All along, it is this reconnection to a meaningful set of sacred dates, your linking directly to the old gods, and making personal and direct communications with them, which will give power and value to your witchcraft. It really has to matter to you that the sun has reached his midsummer zenith, or that the first falling leaf of autumn has reminded you of the time of year. Nature spirituality or today's true paganism is a faith without a book of rules, set feasts, hierarchies of priests, because it is an individual, heartfelt and personal two-way connection with the forces of life.

In England there are a set of times of the year when certain things have been honoured or festivals celebrated. Some of these dates have been taken over by the church, just as they enclosed older sacred sites and kept them as buildings for worship and quiet contemplation. Many old churches have carvings which look very pagan, Green Men, with faces sprouting leaves from mouths, hair or eyes. These are usually taken to represent the Lord of the Forest whose perpetual birth in midwinter, youth in spring, maturity in summer, sacrifice in autumn and rebirth in winter gives an underlying story to modern pagan rituals. There is no historical evidence that the original 12th- to 14th-century carvers thought any such thing, but these beautiful and magical faces with their greenery are so evocative of the living and dying god of Nature.

Many of the depictions of the Virgin Mary, often in stained-glass windows, show her with the symbols of earlier goddesses, and her varied titles link her to these – for example, Stella Matutina is Greek for Star of the morning, actually the planet Venus, often also called Lucifer, the brother of the Moon Goddess Diana. She is the Seat of Wisdom, the gnostic goddess Sophia's title, the Mother of God, the Queen of Heaven, Mystical Rose, Star of the Sea, Tower of Ivory, Gate of Heaven, Queen of Angels, Lady of Earth, and many other names which were attributes of earlier goddesses, Isis, Astarte and Diana. Her image is often shown standing over the sea on a crescent new moon, or surrounded by thirteen stars, usually the five-pointed pentagram, so beloved of wiccans. She often holds a rose for divine love and the traditional symbol of the mystical order of Rosicrucians from whom much magical ritual derives, or the sacred lily, dedicated to Isis, and all virgin goddesses before her.

An aspect of Roman Catholicism which has been adopted by wiccans is the use of the phrase 'Blessed Be ...'. This comes from the Christian rite of benediction or blessing, and begins 'Blessed be God', and goes on through 'Blessed be Jesus' to 'Blessed be the great Mother of God, Mary most holy', and on through a variety of saints. It is used a lot in wiccan initiation and other ceremonies, and as a greeting or closing of letters, and no doubt electronic messages too, these days. It would be better reversed, so that one would simply say, 'Be blessed in the name of our lady ...'

If you are starting to develop your own cycles of seasonal feasts you will need to become aware of the times of the year certain things happen. You should make up your own mind as to whether you want to adopt a rigid, church-like set of fixed dates, need a High Priestess and High Priest, or are happy to acknowledge yourself as a Child of the Great Mother and her Lord, and talk to them, celebrate their life story, make them garlands, sing them spells, and offer them heartfelt thanks when their magic brings you success.

To take the British Isles, for example, if you go through the year, starting in early spring, in the southern part of England, snowdrops usually start to flower around the beginning of February. In warm years it can be as early as the start of January, and in bad conditions, they appear much later. You should take these as a true and living symbol of the Rebirth of Nature, Brigid, the feast of Candlemas, or Imbolc, to give a variety of names. The Goddess is thought to reappear and bring blessings to womenfolk in particular, who decorate 'Bride's Bed' with their finest silks and ribbons, or weave Bridget's Crosses from rushes. Later, the men are invited in to ask their own blessing. What is fixed are the Equinoxes and Solstices, although these too may move a day or two. The Vernal Equinox is usually 20 or 21 March everywhere in the Northern Hemisphere, when the Sun enters the zodiac sign of Aries, and 20 or 21 September in the Southern Hemisphere. This is when day and night are equal in length, and it was traditionally a time of sowing field crops like wheat, although now this is often done in winter. The church's feast of Easter takes its name from Eostra, an old goddess of dawn, and the date varies because it is still fixed by the moon. Easter Sunday is the first Sunday after the first full moon after the Spring Equinox, and many of the traditional symbols seem to have pre-Christian origins. The Easter bunny is the sacred hare, a symbol of the Moon Goddess, and the painted or chocolate eggs indicate the new life springing forth at this season.

As the days lengthen and it gets warmer, the grass grows and hedges turn green. It is the time of the blossoming of hawthorn, the May of May Day, or Beltane, perhaps meaning 'good fire' in the Celtic tongue, and it is celebrated with May Pole dances and the Green Man effigy, a giant found in processions in many places in Europe at this time of year. Some are human giants, others more sinister, like Cornwall's Hobby Hoss, a black circle with a small horse's head which dances in May, accompanied by musicians and other celebrants. May is a time of great expansion in Nature, the blossoming of many fruit trees, and traditional weddings in the green wood. The Goddess and God are married beside the bonfire after magical games of disguise and chasing. Like many human brides in the olden days, to bear her child in December, she would be pregnant at her wedding at the start of May.

Midsummer is the longest day, around 24 June, and bonfires are kindled on hilltops all over the west of England to celebrate. Summer is starting to heat up and flowers and greenery are everywhere, to be woven into sacred garlands. It is when the newly-shorn sheep wandered in the pastures and the fields of corn were beginning to ripen. The Goddess of the Land is at her most bountiful and the god rules over the wild creatures of farm and forest. All the gods of light have festivals around this time, whether they are Lugh or Gwyn ap Nudd or Bran or St John.

As the crops ripen towards Lammas, everyone used to be called in to help with the harvest of whatever grain or other staples were reaped at this time, hence the long school holiday in July and August to cover the corn harvest in many places. If the corn was not cut and brought under cover whole communities could starve, so it was vital that even children played their part, perhaps bringing food and refreshment to the reapers and binders, the stook makers and those who led the carts of sheaves to the barn or rick yard, and built the great corn stacks or hay ricks. Even then the task was only half completed, for the ears of grain had to be threshed from the straw and separated from the chaff, all done by hand until about a hundred years ago. The straw would be saved for thatching roofs or for animal bedding, and the chaff was added to their food. However, even today you can't have an August festival to mark a harvest successfully completed, if the weather has been inclement and the grain still lies rotting in flooded fields or, as in more recent days, it has already been brought in by combine harvester in July.

Many of the Lammas rituals, now held at the beginning of August, recall parts of this practice, the making of Corn Dollies, each woven from odd numbers of long straws with the ears of wheat, barley or rye left on for decoration. Every area had its traditional patterns, and these were tied off with scarlet wool or ribbon and hung above the fire until next year's sowing. Bread was baked from the newly-ground flour to make this a Loaf-mass, from which comes the word, Lammas. Some groups enact the sacrifice of the Corn God who dies, as in the song John Barleycorn, to give life to his people, although barley is roasted and malted and used much more for making beer than bread. The god dies and is supposed to enter into the Otherworld or Underworld until his miraculous rebirth at Yuletide. In some traditions the Goddess, who has been his lover and bride, now becomes a widow, and takes on the darker aspects of old womanhood, including wisdom, intuition and the ability to see into the future. Some rituals reflect these ideas by making the Mourning for Lugh, Lughnassadh in Irish Gaelic.

As we reach the Autumnal Equinox at the old season of Michaelmas, around 21 September, again day and night are equal but now the days are shrinking and the nights are growing longer and cooler. This is a time of balance, signified by the sign of the zodiac, Libra, the scales, but winter is coming and the work of the farms is stepping up again. Now it is the time to gather the fruits, the early apples, pears, blackberries and nuts, the many edible mushrooms and fungi, and herbs to be dried and kept for use in the hungry gap of winter. Cheeses were made, and all kinds of wines, preserves, pickles and chutneys were created with whatever fruits and vegetables were still available, to offer a varied diet when the land was barren. In medieval times the common country folk ate dozens of plants which we now consider to be weeds, like chickweed, sorrel, fat hen, wild garlic, and the early leaves of hawthorn, called 'Bread and cheese' in the spring, which contain a great many minerals and oils essential for health. Stinging nettles were gathered to make beer, the tender young tops could be cooked like spinach or in soup, and the tough stems were retted and beaten to produce a fine yarn or fibre which is like golden silk, used as string and to weave rough hessian.

When the first frosts hardened the land it was time to bring in the cattle and sheep from the higher pastures, and cull those which couldn't be fed through the winter. Their flesh, especially that of pigs, was smoked and turned into hams and bacon, or beef was salted in barrels to feed people during the winter. The fat of sheep, called tallow, was made into simple candles to light people through the dark evenings, until at Candlemas, days were long enough to work through without artificial, if primitive, light. This was the season of Hallowe'en, when the veils between the worlds of the living and dead were thinnest, and you could see into the future and assess the past year. It was a moment of inward looking in preparation for the winter cold, and a final celebration of the harvests that had been gathered. Many old customs, for example, bobbing for apples, the tree of immortality's fruit, or seeing the future in a dark mirror by candle light recall these old traditions, and the ghosts who walked abroad then were those of the family, not only from the past but from the future too.

After the leaves have fallen from the trees and the frosts have silvered the grasslands the year deepens into its winter repose. For farmers there is always something to do now, hedging and ditching, mending equipment, but also telling stories as the families gathered in the warm around the hearth. In the steam from the cauldron, seething over the red embers, tales would be told, and all would follow the action in their mind's eye. Family histories would be recounted and as the days drew in until the depths of Yuletide, it would be a period of assessment and recollection. On the shortest day the Yule log, a great root of oak, would be dragged in and set to burn for the twelve days on the hearth. It would be kindled from the last bit of the previous year's log, to bring luck, health and a sense of continuity to the people. Today, when people have central heating and gas flame-effect fires, the Yule Log has become a chocolate cake complete with plastic robins.

Green boughs of fir, holly, twines of ivy and bay and rosemary would be used to decorate the house. Often a tree branch would be set up and adorned with painted pinecones, nuts or eggshells which pre-date our Christmas tree ornaments. Candles were lit to welcome the coming of the Star Child, the magical Mabon, son of Mother Nature, who, in the darkest hour came to bring light, hope and warmth to the folk in the coming season. People would go out to visit their neighbours, taking small gifts of food and drink, and they would dance and sing carols. The Mummers in certain places would dress up and enact their stories of death of the old and rebirth of the new, with sword fights, doggerel verses and wild over-acting. In Wales, around New Year, the Mari Lwyd, the white mare, a horse's skull decorated with ribbons, and a team of singers would visit the farms, demanding entry. They would challenge those within to a contest of sung insults and scandal.

Yule was not just a day but a period of twelve days, which now run into the start of January, when work was paused on farms and a little fun in a bleak and cold time was to be had. It was an opportunity to teach the young children about the heritage within the countryside, or to tell tales of their ancestors. Some trades took on new apprentices, who were bound to learn their craft over the next seven years. Trades like coopers, the barrel makers, or farriers who shod horses, or blacksmiths who worked iron, might make their new apprentices undergo some kind of initiation ritual in which they were challenged and frightened a little. Even witches would use this still time before the agricultural year took up its cycle again with the first stirrings of spring, to teach their children or novices something of their many crafts. Arts like scrying – seeing visions in a dark glass or bowl of water – are skills that have to be learned, and during the withdrawn period between Hallowe'en and Candlemas there might well be a chance to attempt to master these useful skills. Spinning of wool into cords to use in binding magic, or carving of symbols to use in protective spells could be taught at this time, as well as the learning of the working songs, the chants and the spells of enchantment which empowered witches magic.

Every ritual has a reason, it needs symbols to be set out, mentally or in reality. You may wish to make garlands, or decorate an altar table, blend special incenses, set out seasonal flowers, bake bread, even make your own ritual wines or purifying herbal bath essences. All these things need to be planned well in advance. If you are sharing your work with others, they will need to know what is required of them, and how best to play their parts. Rituals may be celebrations of one of the festivals, but they may also be to divine the future, if you have that skill, with cards, twigs or by scrying. Your rite could mark one of the transitions in life, as at marriage, the blessing and naming of a child, the bidding farewell to a loved one after their death, or the remembrance of those ancestors who have gone before and perhaps been forgotten. You could be celebrating a birthday or anniversary, the coming of age of a young person or the passing into maturity of a grandparent, the achievement of some educational certificate or any of life's milestones which have meaning for your family.

Often festivals need to be pointed at a particular direction, for they may be associated with one of the powers of that direction. For example, a birth, commencement of a project or move to a new home might naturally draw on the powers of East in the dawn of day, the breath of a new life or the cleansing wind which purifies your new dwelling. Marriage is something which occurs in the South, in the eye of noon, when the sun is at his height, to bless and encourage the happy couple, or when you are working solar healing with gold candles and herbs dedicated to the Sun. If you are marking a retirement or the completion of a project, or wish to work on balancing emotions within your magic, in the evening twilight you might set up an altar in the West of the circle. For death, burial or other funeral or memorial ceremonies you might look to the North, where the eternal stars shine in the night sky to remind everyone that nothing is lost from the Universe, it may move or change, but with each death, a new star will shine in the firmament. Rituals involving divination or contacting spirits of Nature might also be worked with an altar placed to the North of the circle, and decorated with evergreens and dark blue or silver candles.

Sometimes you might like to continue this moving theme around the circle of the year. Perhaps you would like to list natural flowers which bloom at each of the major dates, animals which are linked to the festivals, colours, types of incense, things to eat and drink, popular symbols like the Christmas tree, which had its roots in German winter customs before about 1840 CE. You can also look out for pictures of traditional happenings at each quarter and solstice to set out around the sacred date to remind you of the powers other people work with. You can make models of May poles, for example – they don't have to be twenty feet high! Learn to twine garlands out of ivy or willow twigs into which leaves and flowers may be woven, to deck your altar or sacred space. Collect pretty stones, or seashells and interesting bits of wood washed up on the shore, or flat rocks and pinecones which you may find on walks in the countryside. These will all be useful to help you align with each feast as the seasons turn.

You can face a different direction, too, and work your ritual at an appropriate time of day. For example, the Spring Equinox is best celebrated at sunrise on 20/21 March depending on the actual movement of the sun, and it is right to face due East, as that is where the sun will first show himself. At other times his light will creep along the horizon, south in winter and north in summer. At Beltane you can face south-east in mid-morning, and at the summer Solstice face south at noon. Lammas is timed for mid-afternoon, facing south-west, when you should place your garlands of corn and poppies around your altar. The Michaelmas equinox should be pointed to the western sunset, Hallowe'en to the north-west at mid-evening, and Yule to the Pole Star, key point of heaven, at midnight. Candlemas places the altar in the north-east and in the darkness of the early hours of the morning, you should acknowledge the coming of the first flowers and a tiny spark of light, from which all other lamps may be rekindled. The secret feast of Twelfth Night when the wisdom of the Magi was given to the newborn Sun God, symbolically recorded as frankincense, the royal perfume, gold for dominion over the world and myrrh, the scent of sacrifice – all old pagan offerings – is forgotten by wiccans. Then the altar stands just north of east, awaiting the dawn of the new light of wisdom, truth and beauty.

By learning how the turning year brings a new focus to each part of the circle you will discover how cyclical life really is. Of course, you can also weave into this sacred ring the new and full moons, family birthdays and anniversaries, memorial dates and times of luck and good fortune. If you examine this pattern for yourself you will see you have a unique and varied pattern of rituals to develop and perform, with almost one a week, throughout the year. Of course, unless your entire household has also adopted your beliefs you may have orthodox services and festivals to add in as well. Once you open your mind you will discover many ancient aspects to such holidays as Christmas and Easter, Diwali and the Feast of Lights, Thanksgiving and Remembrance Sunday and Hallowe'en. Many modern celebrations have picked up on the currents of Nature and blended rebirth or recollection into their own sacred days. Don't despise other people's feasts or beliefs but look within their customs to see what really does still connect to the spirit of Nature, or a more pagan path, if that is your chosen belief.

Rituals all need an opening when the sacred space is delineated, the powers of the quarters called upon to be present and to protect, participate in and empower your work, and perhaps aspects of the Great Mother and Father may be invited to attend as honoured guests. Then it is necessary to walk around the circle, setting out symbols of the elements or directions if you use these, and generally clearing and making the area magical. After that you should very clearly state the exact intention of that working and stick to it. You can go on to perform the main part of the ritual with words, song, dance, divination, shared activities, the creation of a talisman or the remembrance of times past. There should always be a space for meditation or silence when the Goddess or God might speak to you, or inspire you in some other way. Quiet chanting or singing of traditional songs are another way of allowing other influences to assist you, and some groups use walking meditation when wordless incantations are repeated, bringing a change of consciousness, or circle dancing, if there is enough space.

Later a communion of bread or cake and wine is shared by all visible beings and those unseen presences around you, after the food and drink have been blessed, according to your chosen custom. There may be another quiet moment, or some groups with more formal memberships have a kind of committee meeting or discussion of work to do, or magical successes from the past. When everyone is content that all has been completed, the circles are unwound, and the powers, deities and elemental beings thanked. You have no right to command them to depart, but if you indicate that you have finished what you are doing, you will feel the atmosphere change as the powers return to their normal earthly level. Ensure that everything feels good, that candles have been snuffed out, and that incense is safe. Any sacred items should be carefully cleaned and put away, to ensure they don't get the power that builds up around them dispersed.

Always take time to come to yourself, and never rush a ritual. Hurrying will destroy any chance you have of success, and it is better to work too slowly than too fast, especially if you are a novice. Begin with absolutely simple and straightforward rituals and build in more elements if you feel you need them, as your knowledge and confidence increase. You can't actually do anything wrong, but with practice you can do things better and more effectively! Have a snack, and enter all the details in your Moon Diary as soon as you can, as it is easy to start to forget things that you did or said. Working ritual is often a dream-like experience and you may take a little while to come back to earth. Rushing off in the car, especially if it is late and you are tired, is not a safe or sensible thing to do, so allow a bit of relaxation afterwards. If you are simple, sincere and clear in your desires, the chances are that each ritual will be powerful and successful.

Although I have not just set out the script of a ritual here, because I believe that each ritual should be original and personal to those participating, if you examine the text of this chapter you will see that the framework is clearly spelled out. Arrange your own sacred items, sing your own favourite songs and chants, write prayers, perform dances, make flower and incense offerings in your own special way. Find time within the ritual for silent communion with the beings from the unseen realms of witch magic to speak to you. Work from your heart, with respect, patience and sincerity and those from the beginning of time will hear you and answer. It may be in their own way, and in their own time, but if you have asked clearly and politely, you are bound to be answered.

Nine

THE ARTS AND
CRAFTS OF
THE WISE ONES

He is the true enchanter, whose spell operates not upon the senses

but upon the imagination and the heart.

Washington Irving, *The Sketchbook of Geoffrey Crayon, Gent*

Many of the skills of the witches have to be learned, just as the skills to participate in a sport or play a musical instrument have to be learned. Simple exercises which train the witches' most powerful tool, their minds, have to be mastered by practice and patience. From basic exercises it is then possible to go on to the magical arts of divination, scrying, healing, built on firm and safe foundations.

Witchcraft consists of three things; a reverence for and communion with the Goddess of Nature and the God who rules all wild things; the Crafts of healing, making and mending; and the magical arts of divination, mind travel and spell working. Many modern coven witches seem to deal with only some of these traditional skills and observances, spending more of their time performing complicated rituals under the guidance of a High Priestess or

High Priest, overlooking the vast array of occult arts and skills of their ancestors. What almost everyone knows about witches, whether from television
or from old folk tales, is that they work magic, transform themselves into
animals, fly on broomsticks and can heal or curse according to their current
whim. In fairy stories witches are ugly old women who keep a black cat as a
familiar, often living in an isolated cottage in a wood and being very kind to
children or transforming them into frogs. Some appear as Fairy Godmothers
who grant wishes, cause heroines to fall into enchanted sleep or set impossible tasks when they are in the guise of evil stepmothers.

Perhaps it is time to re-examine some of these ideas and see how many
of the various arts and crafts of modern witches retain something of their
mythical past. Witches work magic by the use of many crafts; some are skills
of hand and brain, like spinning wool in order to weave a spell or bind a difficult problem; or by clairvoyance with a crystal ball or dark mirror. They are
expert bakers, wine brewers, gardeners, embroiderers, painters, poets, metal
and wood workers. They know how to cope with sickness in the body or
the mind, in people and in animals and even in plants. They are observant of
every tiny thing which happens in the world around them, whether it is the
actions of their human neighbours or beings unseen by ordinary people, or
the flights of birds or the growth of plants. Each of these changes is noted and
its importance understood. They are people, both men and women, who can
talk to trees, see the wind, converse with animals and be guided by the stars.
They see in many more dimensions than most people, being able to travel, in
their spirit beings, through both time and space. Some can share the minds
and bodies of animals and plants, seeing the world from a very non-human
perspective. All these skills have to be learned, but every witch will have
some natural abilities as a child.

It is probable that children really understand magic, recalling from former
lives, perhaps, what skills and talents they had. Gradually, as they get older,
the ability to enter into the world of stories or fly in dreams is lost because
their adult minds have to grasp the knowledge of modern life. Many children
and some adults retain memories of these inherited arts, and lots of them
believe in otherworldly beings, whether considered to be aliens or angels.
They accept that magic is real, and that people have the power to do good,
work spells or fly. Anyone who takes up witchcraft as an adult has a lot to

learn, but if you were fortunate to grow up in the country, learning the names of plants, birds, flowers, trees and rocks, you will have a head start over others who have to master this information later in life.

All this basic information has to be committed to memory so that it is readily available wherever you are. Cyber witches soon learn that you can't always take your computer into the wet woods to identify trees, nor will it help you see and talk to elementals or angels. There are many more dimensions of witch wisdom than that found on a flat screen or page. You cannot smell the approach of winter through an image on a VDU, you can't appreciate the sound of flying geese and the touch of the breeze inside a book, nor can you hear the voices of the land or the wind through even the most state-of-the-art electronic speakers. Witchcraft is about being there, having the knowledge in your head and being able, with inner guidance, perhaps, to solve any kind of problem through common sense or magic. Not all difficulties will respond to magic, just as not all illnesses are cured by orthodox medicine.

Witches practised many different healing arts, some relying on a deep and inherited knowledge of the properties of plants. These are not just herbs used in potions, but in lotions and ointments, in soothing teas and sleep-bringing tisanes, in scents and incenses which attract the balancing powers of the air, and in charms, spells and talismans each focused on the needs of the patient. Certain leaves are woven into spells, where their magical rather than medicinal properties are most important, or spell binding may be performed with creepers or whippy saplings, curled into a ring to symbolically surround the problem, and so disable it. Healing of the mind may be encouraged by the patient being lulled into deep relaxation so that the witch may speak directly to their inner selves, seeking a reason for the disease, and then a cure.

Witches heal by laying their hands on sick animals or children who can communicate their pain or distress through touch not words, and they can call upon the assistance of beings from the elements, too, to assist in this art. They have used spiritual healing through words of power, or massage, or more ancient forms of alternative therapies like reiki, shiatsu, acupressure and touch for health. The arts of extracting plant juices with alcohol to make tinctures which are now used in minute quantities in homoeopathy seem to draw on the heritage of 'witch drops', poisonous plant wines used in serious illnesses, with only a tiny dose being given. The knowledge of the healing properties of plants cannot be separated from the knowledge of poisons, for even the most innocent substance given in the wrong dose can have disastrous effects. Most of us think that water is safe to drink, until we fall in a river or the sea!

Witches are trained to keep open the doors of the inner mind through regular meditation. Although it is easiest to learn this art by sitting still, in silence, and allowing new insights to arise into consciousness, in the days when much work was repetitive and boring, witches could meditate as they were spinning wool, hoeing crops, milking cows or walking the dog. We can learn to use time waiting for kettles to boil, or when we are washing up or mowing the lawn in the same way, by opening our deeper senses to inspiration and creative thoughts. By being able to step easily and gently into the world of the mind we can become aware of messages received in waking dreams, or views of the future through reflections in ordinary mirrors. We can become aware of the inner voices of the powers of the elements instructing or helping us find solutions to both occult and everyday problems. Anyone can learn to scry the outcome of magical working in cups of black coffee or lemonade, and those with true sight can do it in hot chocolate or tomato soup!

The wide variety of the old arts of divination seem to have been made much harder these days. Those trying to learn divination with cards have hundreds of Tarot card designs, rune packs, tree, animal or stone oracles to choose from. As well as these, there are fortune telling dice, the Chinese I Ching, and dozens more new systems of divination and prediction. There are instant astrology kits, dowsing rods made of wood, wire, plastic and bone, some basic 'Y' rods, others with counter-weights and hi-tech gizmos requiring degrees in engineering to fathom them out. The old arts of palmistry, tea leaf reading, understanding omens and graphology were probably once the tools of curious witches, who wanted to understand more about their neighbours, or to offer guidance through the labyrinth of life to those who begged for assistance.

Although the idea of spells is widely written about in books these days, few explain exactly how such pieces of old and simple magic are put into practice. Although a spell is actually a set of words, it usually accompanies the making of some kind of traditional charm from natural items. What is hard about spells is that each one is original and only intended to be used once, so each is designed for the exact purpose it is intended for, and nothing else. For this reason 'Spell Books' are not a lot of help to novice witches, unless they are able to see that the spells given are just examples, which can be used as templates for their own work. To make an effective spell you will have to understand things like the powers of the planets, the signs of the zodiac, and all the colours, numbers, flowers and symbols which form the basis of this ancient art. You will also have to be able to compose brief rhyming poems to state the need of the spell and call upon an appropriate deity to bring it into being.

Some spells are to get rid of mice, bad habits or noisy neighbours, others are to attract good luck, health or success, and each is very different. They are all individual because each situation is unique. If the day of the week is different, even if the situation seems the same as another one, there will be differences in the incense used to bless and empower the charm. If a new factor develops in a long-running problem a new spell may be required. To be effective, spells need to define the problem and what needs to be done to fix it, using symbols often derived from the powers attributed to the ten planets. It also has to take into account where those planets actually are in the sky, for this can strengthen or weaken their effects. If one kind of flower is not available you need to know all the possible substitutes, and if a correct number of particular coloured candles cannot be obtained, what do you do then? The experienced witch will have answers as the result of years of work, whereas a beginner might flounder about confused. Practice really is the key.

Because you might want to see what sort of things spells can help with, here are some examples, but they are not intended to be followed exactly as they are written but to encourage you to develop your own ideas.

SPELLSPELLSPELLSPELLSPELLSPELLSPELLSPELLSPELL

A SPELL TO CURE WARTS

Witches were always reputed to be able to cure warts, which are now known to be caused by a virus. If you have warts on your hands or body make sure they are the ordinary sort, by checking with a doctor, as some blemishes on the skin can be symptoms of something far more serious. This spell was designed to be used in spring or summer when dandelions are in bloom.

1 For every wart you will need to pick a flowering stem of dandelion. This exudes a white fluid from the broken end which should be dabbed on each wart to cover it. The fluid darkens to brown as it dries. Do not wash this off for several hours.

2 As you apply the juice sing this chant over every wart: 'Wart, wart, black of heart, I command you to depart. As the flower glows gold as day, take this nasty wart away. In the name of the Lady of the Living Earth, make my skin clear as at my birth. By the healing power of the Lord of the Sky, fade all marks away as time goes by.' Do this *every day* for a week, preferably during a waning moon.

3 You can strengthen this spell by taking a knotted thread of black cotton and touching a knot to each wart in turn, then burning the thread and throwing the ashes into running water. When you know that the spell has worked for you, you may use it to help others, singing with them and helping them tie the knotted threads.

SPELL FOR THE TWELVE DAYS OF CHRISTMAS

This is a different kind of spell, drawn out over twelve days, each of which needs concentration and care. If you miss a day the power of the spell will be broken. You may choose exactly when you begin your experiment; it can be any day between Yule on 21 December to Christmas Day. Yule-tide or Christmas is a time of giving gifts. This is a spell to help you gain inner gifts by giving a small part of yourself each day for the Twelve Days.

1 Each day you will need to follow the same formula, lighting a large candle while you chant the spell, and collecting a token

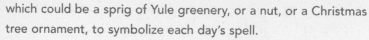
which could be a sprig of Yule greenery, or a nut, or a Christmas tree ornament, to symbolize each day's spell.

2 At some time during each day sing, 'Every day I gain life's gifts, and by this token, I'll repay, when it seems that good luck shifts, to others I'll give it away. With my hand upon the Earth, every day this vow I take, that I will know another's worth, and do my will with no mistake. By the growing power below, and the blessing of the Sky, may my will begin to show, the help I offer, by and by. So may this be!'

3 One day at a time, make twelve promises to be kept, one a month, throughout the coming year, which can be as simple as to speak kindly to a stranger or person who helps you, or to do a specific task which you know will help someone. You must not expect thanks or a reward, as the inner world will repay you when you need it.

4 When you have made all twelve promises, one a day, put the ornaments somewhere safe for the months to come. As you fulfil each promise, remove one token.

SPELLSPELLSPELLSPELLSPELLSPELLSPELLSPELLSPELL

Divination is one of the many gifts that witches encourage, and today most of them have some knowledge of the card oracle, called the Tarot. Using images which go back before the pyramids of ancient Egypt, to the land of Mesopotamia, the cards were first introduced in the form we recognize in the 13th Century. There are four suits, Wands, Cups, Swords and Pentacles with fourteen cards each, and twenty-two extra picture cards with magical meanings. There are hundreds of versions of these cards, some based on the earliest French pattern, which doesn't have pictures on the spot or playing cards, and dozens more, developed since the days of the Order of the Golden Dawn at the end of the nineteenth century, with images on every card.

You will need to spend time learning an interpretation for each card, first upright and then reversed, and then in combination with other cards. This is not the work of a few hours, but rather a task to master, bit by bit, over about a year. It is no good trying to give readings by referring to the book of instructions with the cards, you really need to understand the implications, especially if you are trying to advise someone else. People are often strongly influenced by the turn of the oracle cards, and can be frightened if the reader turns up seemingly difficult images and can't give a true or detailed explanation. Some querents do actually act on what the cards say, so until you are certain what you are doing, only read for yourself.

In order to help you to be a true witch and show wisdom and insight, when you have enough experience, you might find the following spell a help:

SPELLSPELLSPELLSPELLSPELLSPELLSPELLSPELLSPELL

A TAROT SPELL FOR INSIGHT

1 You will need a new Tarot deck and a square of silk, either red or bright blue, and a large surface with a clean flat cloth on it. Open the new pack and, keeping the cards in order, turn them over one at a time. Look carefully at each card, seeing the order in which they are placed. (If you are serious about Tarot divination you will return the cards to this order when you have used them.) Place a tall yellow or gold-coloured candle in a gold-coloured holder and light it.

2 Place the tarot cards face down on the cloth and with both hands, mix them up very thoroughly, saying this spell:

Cards of wisdom, cards of grace, cards with magic on their face,
Open in me the holy power, to answer truly, at this hour.
Open in me the skill of sight, to speak the truth by day and
    night.
Let the knowledge in me rise, that all I say is good and wise.
Help me, Lord of the Tarot.

Clap your hands three times over the cards.

3 Carefully select three cards and turn them over. They will show
   how well your spell has worked by their meanings. These three
   cards will have a real relevance to the subject of your spell, and a
   knowledge of Tarot cards will help you to bring out their magical
   meaning. When you have finished your spell, collect up and sort
   the cards into five piles of suits and Major Arcana, then into
   order. Replace them in their box and wrap it neatly in the silk to
   retain the power which will build up through use.

   Use this spell each time you are doing a serious reading. It is not
   a good idea to let other people handle your special cards, unless
   you are doing a reading for them, in their presence, as outside
   influences can affect the accuracy of any future work, if too many
   people touch them.

SPELLSPELLSPELLSPELLSPELLSPELLSPELLSPELLSPELL

Write down these spells in your Moon Diary and later on look to see what the
outcomes were.

Some of the other arts of witches include various methods of scrying, the
most common way being gazing into an orb of glass or, originally, rock crystal. Witches often used polished pieces of black rock, wet slate or even coal
to scry with, and if it was obtainable the volcanic glass called obsidian made
an ideal speculum or scrying ball. Today people often use a black mirror,
water in a clear glass or silver-coloured bowl, or even a pool of black ink in
a shallow dish. Scrying is difficult because you have to enter an altered state
of consciousness with your eyes open. Most people can obtain visions, like
waking dreams with their eyes shut, but these are very subjective and open
to debate. Images seen in a properly-blessed globe with open eyes will be
clearer and more relevant to the question. This is where all the meditation
practice comes into its own, for it permits the witch to enter the right state
of mind to be able to see with inner sight, but through open eyes. It is not as
easy as it sounds, although, like all aspects of magic, some people can do it
more easily than others.

Here is a simple blessing prayer, which is worth learning and adapting to make it your own, but it is particularly useful if you are going to do any kind of scrying, divination or healing, as you want your mind to be clear, focused on what you aim to achieve and not distracted by random thoughts. This spell can be used before any act of magic, and if you are with other people it helps if everyone uses a similar invocation to bring them spiritually into alignment.

SPELLSPELLSPELLSPELLSPELLSPELLSPELLSPELLSPELL

A SPELL OF GENERAL PROTECTION

1 Light a candle whose colour reflects the nature of the work to be done.
2 Sing or say clearly and firmly but not necessarily loudly:

Lady of Life shine your blessing on me. (Touch top of your head
  with the first and second fingers of your right hand.)
Take my human limits from me. (Touch area of navel.)
Let me find the strength of Light. (Touch right shoulder.)
Let your mercy balance might. (Touch left shoulder.)
All around may wisdom flow, Lord and Lady here below. (Draw a
  circle clockwise through those points, seeing the circle-cross
  pattern light up as a protection around you.)
So may this be, now and forever. (Clasp your hands.)

SPELLSPELLSPELLSPELLSPELLSPELLSPELLSPELLSPELL

Having cast the Spell of General Protection, you may want to use the following scrying technique. You need to have prepared a proper circle to keep out distractions, with the elements set out around the edges, with the glass ball on a black cloth on the north side of a small central table. You need to cut out as much light as you can, and have only one lighted candle to the south which is behind you and cannot show in the surface of the scrying ball. Now focus on one specific question, and ask the powers which govern for clear sight to assist your work. A sweet-scented perfume may be burned, and some old-fashioned witches would blend a mixture of moon herbs in the incense in order that the smoke would help them enter the right frame of mind. By becoming aware of the power of the circle around you, and letting go of all distracting thoughts, you need to focus your eyes within the ball and relax, slowing down your breathing and concentrating on the question. Gradually it will seem as if the glass is clouding over and, after a while, if you can maintain the right level of inner awareness, shapes will start to form. Most beginners lose concentration at this point as they are so surprised that anything is happening. With further work the images, shapes, words, letters, signs and even moving film-like pictures develop until answers can be discovered, or aspects of the future revealed. It can take months of regular practice to get this to happen, for those who do not have a natural propensity for scrying. Even when you get clear images you still have to discover what they mean!

Witchcraft is made up of many skills. Some are quite simple in themselves but they all may have far reaching consequences. Take healing, for example. It isn't all that hard to learn a spell for healing, but do you have the wisdom then, to know when it is correct to apply it? That may take a good deal longer. Do you have the true sense of responsibility which goes with even giving the most basic Tarot reading? That comes only with self-confidence, which in turn can only be learned by practical application. There are many crafts within the Craft and anyone who really wants to be a witch ought to set her- or himself a number of targets to aim for. Achieving these, even on your own, will bring confidence, expertise and effectiveness.

In order to do anything, you need to believe it will have some measurable result – for example, if you make a cake, you will select a recipe, get the right ingredients, carry out the method and cooking as described and, all things being equal, you should end up with a cake. Magic is really very much a matter of the same techniques, especially if you are learning from books instead of within a group or with a personal instructor. You may find a book of spells for all occasions and decide to have a go at one of them. You may be instructed to use a certain symbol, burn a particular incense, invoke a specific God/angel or power on one day of the week. Well, some of these things may be obvious, but others, like the incense or the symbols or even the Names of Power may be strange to you and you aren't certain of their importance or actual meaning. Unlike a cookery book which may suggest you substitute oil for butter or rolled oats for flour, magic books are not so explicit, and it does take years of practice to know what the various alternatives may be.

To become a competent craftsworker used to require a long and complicated apprenticeship, yet many modern witches ask to be taken on and initiated into a coven as a first step, rather than as the culmination of many years of training and learning. Before an apprentice shipwright was allowed to place a plank on the hull of a new ship he would spend years, perhaps, making the tea for the craftsmen, watching their every move, and learning how they tested the curve and strength of the wood, the pattern of the ribs and the final lines of the completed boat. This applied to any trade. The apprentices watched and began with the simple jobs, sweeping the workshop, replacing the tools, asking 'fool' questions until they intuitively knew they were ready and able to begin on the real work. Their inner senses of the 'rightness' and 'feel' of a piece of material, a tool or a plan were ingrained into them long before they were allowed to show what skills they had mastered in practical terms.

The Arts of the Witches fall into four categories: practical skills like herbalism and talisman-making; magical arts like divination and spell-working; 'psychic competence' and inner vision; and personal/religious worship or contact with the Goddess/Gods. Many of these can be read about in books and practised quite safely on your own, or with another novice-friend. You must try to hold a clear idea of what you aim to achieve and begin simply with one or two arts. Learn by heart a meaning for every Tarot card, not directly from a book, but by examining the picture or implications from your personal standpoint. That will take a few weeks! Perhaps you fancy a crack at dowsing, so make a pendulum and get used to its reactions for Yes/No or Positive/Negative which may be equally individual to your own psyche.

Work on your own inner skills and the things which you already have some confidence about. No one is going to seek healing from an individual who always looks unwell, or is clearly suffering from some illness or disadvantage. Be prepared to seek help – alternative healers in many different disciplines are becoming more and more readily available and they can often find solutions to long-standing problems, allergies or other upsetting symptoms. If you have consulted a homoeopath or an aromatherapist, an osteopath or a reflexologist, you will be able to see how alternative forms of healing are applied and this may influence you when you begin to work on behalf of others, either by physical therapies or magical ones. If you are on the receiving end of the correct alternative therapy it will make you feel much better and this, in turn, will release energies which can help with your inner and outer life. By becoming fully well you will be less of a burden to the Earth Mother, the Great Goddess herself, whose child you are. You may well find out, too, that nature can heal you, and by learning how, you can exploit the gifts of nature to heal others.

Do learn to 'switch off the world' by any reliable form of meditation – this does take constant and regular practice and you will never be able to hear the voices of the Great Ones unless you have learned to be still and listen. In times past people didn't talk about 'meditation', but they day-dreamed, mused and, like William Davies' tramp, knew, 'What is this life if full of care, you have no time to stand and stare.' During boring and repetitive jobs, like hoeing crops or picking up stones or mowing hay, there was a steady rhythm to which you would work and ponder.

By learning about what our forebears did, what family job they followed, we may still be able to learn magics from the past. The Craft was a craft, it was made up of just as many varied skills and bits of inherent knowledge as the trade of carpenter, shoemaker or mystical blacksmith. The Guilds and Lodges of the Craftsmen preserved both the arcane philosophy and the practical trade secrets of their craft so that standards of workmanship and the identification of Fellow Craft members was secured by passwords and gestures, as it is today.

Magic of any kind requires a great deal of self-assurance and confidence and to a novice, working alone at some strange technique or art, this can be a very great step. In some ways, it is a good deal easier for the beginner-witch than it is for, say, the novice Qabalist, because at least part of the Craft is concerned with a religious belief in the Old Gods/Goddesses. The Qabalist may well believe that the power to work rituals and achieve results by complex symbolism is something to be mastered under the kindly tuition of a convenient adept, and so delay the start of any practical work, possibly, for years even, but the witch will want to begin at once, try out her skill at divination, or make up a seasonal celebration for her family, perhaps.

Many of the books written about witchcraft these days are concerned with covens, festivals and arts, rituals and celebrations which were designed for groups of at least six people. There is an alternative older, simpler and lonelier path which many a village witch has trodden through the ages, but nothing has got as far as print, although there are a few handwritten books on the subject. Here each witch is in direct touch with her own aspect of the Goddess and God of Old Time. The rites are often those of a whole village or community, held out of doors on a special date when everyone dances in the streets, decks their houses with a branch of new green leaves, or wild flowers, according to season.

The magic of these popular festivities is the secret, kept within the minds and acts of those 'in the know'. It is the flowers round their front doors, or the posy they cast into the bonfire, the pattern of their dance steps or the weaving of their corn dolly which preserves and encompasses the magical part of the public celebrations. This goes on to this day, and the special participant will reply, 'We have always done it this way,' or 'That's the way it's done,' when you ask why their acts are different. They may not now know the full significance of the actions that have come down to them through the family, but they are ones who are preserving very ancient links with the Gods and Goddesses of Old. Britain is a fortunate land in that, though many old celebrations did get lost and banned during the years of the Commonwealth, many did survive the critical 60-year gap and were revived, and others are still being rediscovered from local records and folk memory. We may have lost a lot of our maypoles and fertility rituals but equally much has lived on in small villages and in the songs and dances of the country folk.

Learn about your history, family, location and land. Each is full of important bits of magical and mythical lore. The landscape was influenced long ago by people who built earthworks or set up stone circles or carved great white sacred figures from the chalk hillsides, because these had an important social, religious or magical purpose. By attuning your stilled mind to those far-off folk you may revive their arts, their skills and discover their motivations. The landscape is full of mysteries which science may not be able to solve, yet the flexible and wide-ranging mind of an interested would-be occultist may succeed. It is getting easier, using the internet and pooled family records to trace who your ancestors were, and even if you don't know them, you carry a long heritage of their genetic make-up. You may even have reincarnation memories from other members of your family, recorded in your genes.

Examine aspects of your own intents to find areas where you do feel quite confident and gradually expand these in magical directions. Obviously, if you feel very unsure of yourself you aren't likely to launch yourself, alone, into a complicated ritual full of strange words of power and intricate symbols. It is important to begin your ritual work with something within your own grasp. Start off with a simple ritual of thanksgiving, saying a heartfelt 'thank you' for a gift of good health, a bit of luck or the success of some dream. You don't need to know the various names of the Goddess/Gods, just address your invocations to the Lady of Luck, or the God of Good Health. They will know, and you may make your first tentative contact with them as living and communicative beings of a different order to our own. Seek out wild places where the Goddess of Nature may show her face unveiled.

Look at the many calendar customs or seasonal festivals which are based on the Sun moving from one sign to another at the solstices and the equinoxes. The exact times can be found in an ephemeris, a book of tables from which all astrologers derive their data. These are very useful because you can quickly learn on which days the planets will be in helpful or difficult alignments for any magical purpose, all of which have some planetary links. Ephemerides also tell the exact position of the moon and at what precise moment she is full or new – a fact which really matters in magic. The other, older cross-quarter festivals – Candlemas, Beltane, Lammas and Hallowe'en were originally set by the agricultural activities in the land itself. You can't celebrate the harvest when the corn is still green, nor the coming of lambs if they aren't to be born for weeks or months. May Day is when the hawthorn in your area is first in flower, from late April in southern England to probably June in Scotland. You can't celebrate in a grand way until you understand what is being celebrated! Get on with your homework – spend a while noting down the first flowering of snowdrops for Candlemas, the first day of

Harvest for Lammas in your area. Watch the trees coming into leaf and the activities of wild birds in your garden. Build up a feeling of how to react to the seasons, as the sacred flowers of your land blossom.

See how you feel as the Moon changes her phase – are you more sensitive and psychic at the new or full moon? Do your dreams become clearer, does your body react differently – when are your high and low times? (You need to know this so that you don't do healing work when you are low or try to divine or work magic when things are not at their best). Which season do you prefer? How does diet, environment, company affect you? What things make you feel really good and lively, and what makes you dull? These are all matters any witch will be interested in, for they all see themselves as guinea pigs to experiment on. If you have successfully tried a cure or a technique, or cast a spell, you will be able to thoroughly recommend it to someone else.

Consider how you feel about being called a witch, or a pagan or a member of the Craft. Think what it might feel like to be rejected by your friends and family, few of whom will understand your interest, especially if you lock yourself away to meditate, or change your diet and habits. It is far better to come to terms with what the neighbours will say before you admit to joining a coven, attending sabbats and collecting swords, athames and all the other bits and pieces some writers consider essential to the occult arts. You will get some weird looks when you tell folk you can read the Tarot cards, and you will get requests if you admit to practising healing. You must be competent and act responsibly in all these fields before you let the world know, both for your own sake and theirs. There is no excuse if people take your advice on their health or future and find you were wrong!

This is why magic still has its secrets. It is why success comes instantly only after several years of practice, and it is why those who are best thought of in the magical world are simple, unaffected by the power they wield, and usually wealthy only in terms of self-assurance and self-confidence. In any magical skill common sense is far more important than a big bank balance. Read all the books you can but do so in a critical way – think what sort of person the author might be. Study information about Nature and her many varied gifts of inner vision and outer art. Ignore no source of knowledge but apply practical thought to it. Learn to rely on your own feelings, develop your skills slowly and carefully, admitting nothing until you understand your art and your responsibility to others.

Make friends with the Goddesses/Gods and don't be overwhelmed by other peoples' claims to fame or ability. Learn to trust your own intuition so that you can see clearly in a divination, and know from inner experience that a cure or spell will work. Hasten slowly, helping in small ways until you do have the confidence in your art and the forces of Nature. You alone can decide your path in the Craft, but do be willing to tread it alone rather than joining the first group that you come across. Inner sight will be clear and intuition will lead you to those companions who are on your wavelength, and these will be worth waiting for. True confidence comes only from knowledge, and in turn that comes from experience. Build up your own strengths, be patient and you will surprise yourself!

Get to know your dreams so that the hidden messages your subconscious mind is sending you are received each morning. This, combined with meditation and arts of clairvoyance, will make you a powerful magic worker and teller of the future. By discovering what talents you have and then developing these, you will begin to be able to map your own position in witchcraft. Certainly covens do have sets of three degrees which are given by separate initiations, but even going through a ceremony with other competent people doesn't mean you will immediately be able to scry, heal or know one herb from another. Such powers cannot be given, they have to be earned and then recognized in retrospect. By acknowledging your own powers and worth, and by developing skills and giving yourself credit which no one else can do, you will strengthen your self-confidence and abilities. Take small steps along the path of practical magic and witchcraft and gradually you will find your talents unfolding, so that insights, guidance and knowledge are at hand when you need them. Learn to trust your intuitions, feelings and those flashes of true wisdom which will increasingly show you are gaining control over your witchy self. It can be a long road, but the use to your world and community is enormous.

Perhaps you will find it is necessary to look back, even two or three generations within your family, if you want to discover what magical or healing skills you might have inherited. See how different things must have been, how much harder, more controlled and inward-looking the way of life of your

ancestors, two or three generations ago. There was no travel to foreign lands
– going to a town miles away could be a once-in-a-lifetime adventure. There
were no groups or committees, gatherings or societies in which people shared
their interests. Church was where you saw the others in your community,
especially if it was a scattered rural one, rather than an urban sprawl which
many of us live in today. There were no covens of bakers, convents of priests,
lodges of masons, nor any other sorts of groups following the same occupation or craft, except the trainees within the family group. Covens don't really
fit historically into the social web as it was a hundred years or more ago.

We are used to school classes, clubs and gatherings for all kinds of purposes and we are free to associate where and with whom we choose. Our
ancestors were not, nor did they live in a society in which meetings or getting together was an accepted part of their lifestyle. Folk met at church or the
market place, for there were few shops, or at seasonal fairs or processions.
They might gather at hiring fairs or local celebrations at Harvest Home but
it was a rarity rather than an everyday event. We are all constantly in touch
with other people, even more so now when mobile phones connect individuals to discuss trivia all the time. In the past everyone lived a much more
independent life, cocooned in silence before the electronic cacophony came
into being. Silence was and is golden, for it is the gift of the Lady of Silence
whose quiet voice can only be heard when other sounds sleep. It is the speech
of wisdom and the tongue of insight that modern gadgets blot out, but which
today's witches must make space to hear.

Many of the practical Crafts were learned by observation from other members of the family or village, just as, in the days before TV, children saw the
activities of their parents and copied them. Toys used to be miniature versions
of tools or cooking pots, or dolls with which the youngsters imitated their
mothers' activities. Today it can be very hard for us to look back to even the
start of the last century when life was so different; without electricity, heating,
radio and TV, washing machines and vacuum cleaners. But it is from those
simpler roots that the powers, festivals and wisdom must have come to bring
to us, at the start of the twenty-first century, information on witchcraft
and magic.

Ten

DEITIES, SHRINES AND THE PATH AHEAD

Religion is like a candle inside a multicoloured lantern. Everyone

looks through a particular colour, but the candle is always the same.

Mohammed Naguib, News summary, NN USA public broadcast, 31 December 1953

Creating a magical space, in or out of doors, learning how to decorate it, and using it as a focus of magic can be a valuable process for everyone, no matter what their state of faith or belief. You will find that developing a personal calendar of sacred dates and special occasions or discovering ways to mark 'rites of passage' adds meaning to the passing seasons in your own life. From self-analysis you will learn how to deal with loss or success, how to seek inner counsel or far sight, and through working within a sacred space or circle you will find comfort and strength.

The Craft has had a long history of disapproval at the mildest and outright persecution at the most destructive. Always it has been people who have attracted attention to themselves who get the worst treatment, both historically and even today, when their motives or actions are questioned. There is no way that any group, be they witches or ritual magicians or occult practitioners of any sort can demonstrate their work for the good of others. If they do demonstrate healing rites or beneficial magic in public their accusers have only to say, 'Oh, yes, that is what they showed us, for the cameras, or during the interviews, but we know [usually on very spurious hearsay], that really they sacrifice animals and put curses on people.' You can never put up a case against that sort of wild rumour, or convince those who are certain, even on no evidence at all, that all witches and pagans are devil worshippers and performers of nameless horrors in their magic rites.

There is only one defence against such criticism. It is old and, for many people, it is extremely hard, but it is a traditional part of all magical initiations, and today's witches ought to know about it. That defence is 'Silence'. According to one oath which is quite popular with modern covens, the new witch, 'in the presence of the Mighty Ones, do of my own will and accord most solemnly swear that I ever keep secret and never reveal those secrets of the Craft which shall be entrusted to me.' Now that means something. Whether you work alone with the Goddess, or within a coven which can trace its roots right back to the Ice Age, or a newly-formed training group, somewhere along the line, you will have to take an oath. It may not be the one quoted here (that one happens to be public), but whatever you say, it has meaning, and part of that meaning is that you do not advertise your 'witchness' to outsiders. It usually only leads to trouble, not necessarily just for you, but for anyone you may be involved with.

It is necessary, for your own safety and that of your colleagues, to find a way of indicating that you are a committed pagan or witch but in such a way that the nosy-parker or antagonistic individual will not be aware of the symbolism. Of course, those inside the Craft or Magic will be able to recognize you by the light in your eyes and the shine in your aura, as you should know well, but there is a vast array of traditional things you can do to indicate your allegiance to others. You will have to use your intuition to discover these.

If you have decided to become a 'pagan' or a 'wiccan' and you want to 'come out' by announcing your change of status to the world at large, how will you do it? People will laugh at you, they will probably make uninformed or rude remarks. The least you can expect is a limp 'Oh, really?' and a change of subject. At the other end of the spectrum of response there could be outright hatred, fear, distrust and the start of a deteriorating relationship which could have far-reaching effects in your job and your home life. Scandal-mongering is a popular hobby with the uninformed and ignorant – take a glance at certain aspects of the popular press, if you want confirmation of that. Often it is best to say nothing until you are sure those around you value you as a person, and will not be perturbed by anything you might say about your faith. Any rash statement cannot be retracted or altered, and some people are highly opposed to any minority.

The same care should be taken if you intend to perform small magical workings or rites in public places. There has never been any bother, calling in of the Law, or interference at all to casually arranged seasonal celebrations. On one occasion a bunch of magical friends of mine were happily celebrating on top of a fairly remote Welsh hill when a Sunday School party hove into view. Instead of rushing into our circle and kicking over the sacred items and flowers or making rude remarks the children held back. Their teacher quietly said, 'Come away, children, they are holding a service ...' and they all departed out of sight. When we saw them later in the day they were quite friendly and we wished each other 'Good day.' True we weren't in fancy dress, but some of the company did have staffs and we were burning incense which is not common in Welsh Baptist chapels. Certainly the Goddess looks after her own.

Magic is a chameleon art, able to change and hide, even in plain sight. It has never gone away but it will certainly have changed through the turning years. We have the threads in our hands now, but how many of those who try to pass on these timeless crafts are refashioning them in plastic and other modern materials? If you want to make contact with the Earth Mother do not buy a man-made model of some classical sculpture, go out and touch the ground. Lean on a living tree, created by the Mother of All, from the same star-stuff that we are made of. Look at the Moon, watch her phases, learn the movements of the planets and the patterns of the constellations so that you can see when Jupiter is in Virgo by observation. It is no substitute to use a digital watch with moon phases. To use the power of the Moon which surges with the tides of the sea, flows in our own blood, and causes weak mushrooms to push through inches of concrete, you must see her, eye to eye. All these are valuable assets to magical work.

If the part of witchcraft which most interests you is the pagan religious aspect then you should make it part of your research and activities to find out exactly what goddess you are worshipping, or which aspect of the god you are asking for help. It isn't good enough to simply follow the words of a book, just because it is in print. You need to be aware that the 'names' of Deities are job descriptions with a meaning and purpose, and not just names. If you want to call upon the Goddess in a particular aspect you are much more likely to be able to see her and commune with her if you address her in your own language, asking to become aware of the aspect of healing, peace or Earth.

Most of the published god names are foreign. Most countries and traditions have had perfectly valid goddess and god names for thousands of years. There are plenty of recent books on Celtic myths and legends and some students have taken to using the names of heroes and heroines from that source as god/goddess names, but take care. You may well not want to call upon a giant, a bird or a pig when you are making a supplication. You owe it to the Great Ones to find out what they call themselves, from them, rather than guess or use wrong or unacceptable material. After all, the Old Ones know your proper name, even your true inner name, which you may not yet have discovered! You should treat them with respect and honour.

The ancient deities were attached to particular places, because the Wise Ones of Old had encountered these Gods at that particular place. They didn't erect a shrine or temple and then call upon the gods to be indwelling, they walked around with their inner sight open until an oracle or an epiphany showed them a place and which Deity was attached to it. Then they asked what sort of sacred shrine needed to be made there, and only then, did a place become sacred to people. Many of the oldest holy sites do not have any kind of building upon them. The creation of temples and then churches began with the Greeks and Romans who wanted to solidify and identify their Gods and holy places, and then show off their imperial wealth to pilgrims. The Great Ones do not require roofs, they are too big; they do not require walls they only need recognition, within a quiet body, a dedicated heart and the common sense to go to the places, on Earth, they inhabit.

The Ancient Deities were originally (and still are for that matter), not people. They are not in human form, seen in antique costumes hugging some symbolic object, or dressed in the fashions of some cult. They are vast and mighty independent forces, formless, timeless, yet powerful and able to hear us and help us, nonetheless. It is human insensibility which has tried to call them into houses, encase them in human form and clutter them with mythology to try to understand them. They are really not the way that the sculptors of ancient Greece and Rome depicted them, as superhumans with all the faults of human beings – the greeds, lusts and failings. They are forces, powers, light, creativity, none of which can really be envisaged as dressed up people. We have inherited a false image, and now make it worse with idolatry, putting images in place of Nature on altars in rituals, conducted in houses. Yes, I know many witches today live in cities, but you still have windows, maybe even gardens, you can grow pot plants, filled with the Life Force, which is a far more true essence of the Living Mother of Earth than a plaster Venus. It is this continual distancing from Nature and the Moon Goddess/Earth Mother and Sun/Sky Gods which makes this kind of indoor paganism unreal.

If you really feel drawn to actually worship, ask for help, offer thanks or request healing or any of the other things which the Old Ones will certainly grant freely, please make the effort, if only for a moment of time, to go out under even the densest city sky, and make contact. Take a few deep breaths to link you with the All Living Ones, feel the earth beneath your feet, smell plants or trees or just those subtle scents found in the air which tell of the season. Autumn is the most obvious, but you can smell Spring or Summer if you try.

Do think about your actions. What would the ideal be? To live in a remote rose-covered cottage with its own well, on a sacred site no one else knows about? Perhaps it is! If you investigate the area in which you live there may be a local well or spring, now underground, there may be a legend of a sacred tree, a magical rock, a healing grove just where your brick-built house is now. If you travel through time, whilst remaining in the same place, and the Goddess who is Time will certainly help if you ask her, you might discover that under your garden there was the idyllic farmland and woods that you desire to be in. If you don't perceive your Deities as having anything to do with actual Nature, why are you trying to be a pagan?

If you are not able to get to such idyllic surroundings you will have to fall back on what you are able to create, for the occasion, either outside in your garden, or inside your home. You may be able to arrange a more permanent shrine where you live, so that you can set out the leaves or flowers, models or pictures of animals or symbols you associate with the time of year. Ideally a table set in the corner of a room can be used, draped with a clean cloth whose colour links it in your mind to the current season. Here you can set out potted, living plants, rather than cut flowers, even bonsai trees or seedlings, elegant pieces of rock, curved and interesting branches, sea shells, pebbles, and other treasure trove that you have collected on your magical journeys. Because certain times of the year are associated with the activities of animals, both domestic and wild, you might like to start a collection of postcards, for example. This is particularly useful if you have children who are interested in the turning seasons, as they can help set out the flowers and other objects.

You might like to have symbols of the zodiac and a golden model of the sun, or silver copies of the phases of the moon, to remind you of her phase if the sky is cloudy or, because she is waning, she rises too late to see. Many witches gather all sorts of candlesticks and lamps, incense or oil burners so that they can use a little of their favourite perfume each day. This shrine can be a focus of your meditations, not only as something to look at, but also as its position can mark the edge of an imaginary, protected circle where your personal and individual rites may take place each day. By regular work and attention to the shrine it will build up power, so that a charm or talisman placed there will be empowered, or be assisted to work more swiftly, by the surrounding influences. However, such shrines should not be worshipped, but rather seen as signposts of the time, or pointers to what is needed to be worked on. This is why I have not suggested you have statues of gods and goddesses, because as living beings of Earth and sky they are near you all the time.

Old-fashioned witches were always aware of the season, phase of the moon and often the planetary position, in their daily lives, and didn't need objects or idols to remind them. Unlike some faiths, pagans can see their deities all the time, when they look at a garden, or watch the sun in the heavens. You will have to discover for yourself what form these great living beings may take, by asking them to appear in your dreams and visions. The images of many of the gods of classical times were decided by a priesthood, who gave the carvers of statues idealized human forms to take as a starting point, and then added the particular symbols that relate to their divine form. Jupiter or Jove has his thunderbolt, Venus or Aphrodite has her bow or mirror, the many gods and goddesses of ancient Egypt have human bodies and sacred animal heads, to show they were greater than human beings. If you do use statues be very sure to know who you are actually dealing with and be certain that that particular deity has the qualities you need. Many goddesses were rulers of war before they became bearers of harmony or a happy home life!

You may prefer the deities to be symbolized by light or wind or coloured shapes seen in the sunset sky. They can be felt as forces, or perceived as invisible energies of power or emotion or simply transformation. You can worship unnamed gods and goddesses by giving them your own titles, like Lady of Love, God of Growing Things, Ruler of the Tides of Time and so on, if you have a particular concept which you wish to contact. It is far safer than trying to use names you have got out of books, because you won't know all their attributes. Also, *never* mix deity names from different traditions, even if it sounds wonderful. Each group is part of a natural pattern and will produce harmonious and powerful effects. Mix traditions and you will get disruption, chaos and trouble, and it will spill over into your dream life, if you are not careful. Each set or pantheon of gods grew up in the same place, to represent different facets of the original creative spirit and to complement each other, work together and share symbols which come from the same root. In a mixed set, several may share a symbol but be completely opposite in effect. Do be careful, and if you aren't sure, just say 'Holy Mother' or 'Divine Father' or something equally simple, and you can't go wrong.

To decorate your shrine, especially if it is out of doors, you might like to make garlands of natural greenery and flowers, adding berries, seeds and pinecones depending on the season. You will need some thin and springy twigs like willow or hazel, to bend into a circle about a foot across. You can use a wire coathanger or florists' wire as a base if necessary, but natural things can be left as an offering until they fall apart without harming wildlife. Over the basic circle you can twine ivy or other creepers, or pad out the circle with moss, thinner twigs and long grass stems. These materials can be soaked in water and then flowers, buds, stalks of green leaves or autumnal colours can be added for seasonal effect. Even fruits including small apples, rose hips, hawthorn haws and wild fruits may be entwined or stuck into the ring to become food for birds and animals. Use short twigs to hold pine cones or other decorative natural materials in until the whole circle is covered. These may be hung on a stang, or forked witches' staff, or from the branches of a tree during your rituals. Indoors they could be hung from a hook in the ceiling of your shrine, or on the wall behind it. Miniature versions could be worn on your head, or less stiff materials used to make garlands with flower heads and leaves to wear round your neck, or for invited guests at your festival, or to offer to Mother Nature during rituals out doors.

You might like to mark out your sacred circle on the ground with leafy branches, laid in a ring, or stuck upright to delineate your area of power. Once this is blessed it should be seen as impregnable, and to leave you will have to deconstruct it, or make a bridge or gap to pass through. When you become more sensitive you will see the circle as a ring of living light, and know it will fend off distractions both as physical intrusions and as any chaotic energies which are around. It is not necessary to perform heavy banishing rituals when working witch magic because you want to make friends with the forces of Nature, not drive them away. Some may feel strange when you first encounter them, but you will become more confident that you are safe, and that such meetings are beneficial, as you go along. If you start trying to drive away influences you don't yet recognize you may cut yourself off from ever-developing increased perceptions which are essential to witchcraft. Be a bit daring, but also use common sense to decide what is sensible to do.

The Circle created in magical work, whether alone or with a group, should actually be seen and felt as if it is between the worlds. You should see not your garden or front room, but the sacred grove, the holy hill, the inner Temple of the Old Ones, built of dreams, prayers and desires. The people around you should be their true pagan selves, enhanced from their everyday selves, because that is what magic is about. Many of those who have been trained in ceremonial magic will be well aware of the inner temple, of creating a magical personality, of seeing with enhanced vision, but lots of witches I have talked to don't seem to have been taught these things. Once you have visited a place in the real world you can create it mentally in your meditations to use as an inner shrine or background to your magic. Call up the image, bit by bit, allowing the sounds, sights, atmosphere and weather to build slowly around you, until it is real. Hold this during your ritual, and with practice, you will find you can maintain the inner circle even with your eyes open.

Whatever you do, become thoroughly aware of what you are actually using, what any symbols, pictures or images are there for. If you are just going by the words of some book, think hard about its writer, what did he or she really believe, see, intend that you should learn or do as a result of the words? Each generation of worshippers seems to degrade what they receive from the previous generation, missing out bits they don't understand, or dogmatizing rules and regulations. Some witches go by the calendar, and not by the very blessing of the Goddess they purport to worship. I know that groups have to meet on set days, usually at weekends, but each individual is still free to worship alone, the moment the Goddess or the God reveals the power of the season to them! You can talk to the Great Ones outside a magical circle without a High Priestess there to hold your hand, if you seek them in their own realm, and that is where the signs of the seasons are, not on the calendar.

If you are alone, how might you find companions on the various paths of witchcraft and other magics these days? Often it is best to start with physical rather than virtual contacts, because though electronic information sources may be vast, they are also uncontrolled. In every country there are a number of small, specialist magazines on witchcraft, astrology, fortune telling, earth mysteries or magic and from these it is possible to discover possible further steps. When witchcraft first reemerged from the shadows in the 1950s and 1960s, there were few public points of reference. In 1964 the editor of the magazine *Pentagram* organized a dinner in London for about 50 people who were interested in witchcraft and magic. That was the first such meeting ever held, and since that a number of annual conferences have been arranged by different organizations. The oldest conference, run by my magazine *Quest*, began in 1968, and has continued each year in March since then.

Lots of magazines have been published, some lasting only a few issues, others becoming glossy regular journals, available all over the world. Others remain small circulation, privately-produced, subscription-only publications, but these are often mentioned in the bigger magazines if you look. Many towns and cities now have 'New Age' shops which sell books as well as Tarot cards, incenses and other supplies for those seeking spiritual enlightenment. Both the shops and the small magazines often list training schools, open conferences, festivals, rituals and other gatherings, large and small, all around their country of origin. You will have to use your own discretion when you follow up these clues, but on the whole, any organization which declares itself in print must be traceable and accountable to the magazine, if not the larger magical community. Such people are carefully policed, magically and morally, and the ethics of witchcraft are extremely high.

If you want to contact a local coven, that is a different matter. Wiccan groups are nearly all independent and small, the average coven may have less than thirteen members, and none will admit people for initiation until they are eighteen years of age. Some groups offer training at regular 'Outer Court' meetings, where their philosophy and intentions may be explained. A few wiccan writers run courses in person or by correspondence, which give new-comers a chance to grasp the basic skills and knowledge. Here and there, individual old-fashioned witches take on a few apprentices, and put them through tough training courses, usually lasting many years, to instil into them all the country knowledge, wild wisdom and spiritual disciplines that are required for effective witchcraft.

In Britain there is the Pagan Federation, the largest mainly pagan organi-zation in the world, which, since the 1970s, has gradually expanded from a handful of witches to include a large number of people from all traditions and walks of life. Through quarterly magazines, local and regional conferences, and a large annual gathering each autumn, they bring together seekers and teachers, writers and magazine editors, suppliers of equipment, robes, incenses and other materials, to exchange ideas and make introductions. Many of the participants are initiated wiccans, witches and pagans of other paths, and plenty of opportunities are offered to meet and make new contacts. Some of these can lead to individuals finding the kind of group they wish to join. On the whole, those who want to be admitted to a coven will first have to find one, then go through that coven's particular process of developing mutual trust and liking, training and respect, before admission, usually by some kind of initiation ritual. Some covens will seek out suitable people at public meet-ings, others offer basic training, from which candidates must seek admittance to the coven by approval of the High Priest and High Priestess.

In America there are a number of widely-read magazines which list meet-ings, suppliers and courses from which further steps may be taken. Usually it is up to each individual would-be witch to discover a path for her- or himself to the group or tradition they feel they most want to follow. Although some covens seem to have binding oaths which suggest that once inside you can never leave, really those who wholeheartedly commit themselves to witch-craft will find they have no wish to depart, although they are actually free to leave a group or tradition at will. No one has the right to demand personal and undying allegiance, no matter what they may say. Again, a first step is often to attend open conferences and seasonal celebrations and see if you like the people you meet. If they like you, you will receive invitations to take your spiritual journey further.

Covens also have three degrees, and wiccans may progress at different speeds according to how much work or commitment they are able to give their Craft. Some groups use sexual rituals, usually between live-in partners, as part of the third degree rite, or on other occasions if their tradition demands it. Be very careful to ask about this, and do not get involved in anything you feel uneasy about. Saying 'No' can preserve your health and dignity, and a better opportunity will always come along. Always be sensible, especially if you are young or inexperienced in life. There are nasty people who call themselves witches, just as there are priests or doctors or therapists who do not live up to the high ethical standards of their chosen path, but there are probably less unethical witches and wiccans about. This may be because they believe in karma and reincarnation. You can't get away with unlawful behaviour forever, and the Lords of Karma, the angels who control such aspects of human fate, are eternally watchful and able to exact payment for any harm done.

Always act with care, whether you are requesting a Tarot reading at a New Age fair, or seeking initiation into a group where you don't know the other people. Treat any information you are given with caution, and always listen to your own heart and feelings rather than being swept away by what is being told to you. People who claim high titles, years of experience or secret magi-cal knowledge could be trying to entrap you into something you would rather not be part of, and it is best to leave time to consider any offer before committing yourself. If people ask you to keep what you are told secret, consider the implications. It is traditional never to give the names of other members of any magical working group, coven or lodge to casual enquirers, nor the time and place of meetings. Many groups keep the special names they give to their Gods and Goddesses under wraps, as well as any magical names, titles, degree levels or achievements of their various members, and this knowledge should be treated with respect and discretion. However, if you are expected to do things you feel uneasy about which you may never mention to anyone, be very careful, and if possible find someone you can discuss it with. If you don't know many witches, you can always write to the editor of a magical magazine or to a book author via their publishers for advice.

If you are expected to choose a magical name, consider what this may imply. Beware of adopting elaborate titles like Lady Aphrodite Unicorn, or Lord Thoth of Avebury Covenstead, which some wiccans plaster all over everyday correspondence. It is better to be more discreet, and not to select god or goddess names as your own, except perhaps Daughter of Diana or Son of Cernunnos. If you take the name of a deity, and that force is invoked, so may you be, and it is likely that the human with the name is nearer than the divine one! Consider all these ideas carefully, and recognize that even alone, as a complete beginner or relative novice, you can learn the arts of witchcraft, gradually developing power, confidence and psychic sensitivity, so that you will know who to call upon, how to set up a sacred space, celebrate a festival, recognize the symbols of the Tarot cards, or the planets in the sky. No one is too young to begin to learn about plants and about themselves, for true witchcraft is within, and can be expanded as a gift from Mother Nature and the Lord of the Wild. No one else can truly initiate you, and if the gods do accept your service, no one can empower you unless you take responsibility for the control and effects of that power. It is always the deities who make witches, not other people; after all, who made the first witches?

It does help a lot if you have a sense of humour too. Don't ignore the 'wit' in witchcraft! Most of the truly effective witches have been able to see the funny side of events if things go wrong, to laugh at themselves and serve their deities with a light heart and a sense of fun.

Lilith of the Enterprise Coven,

At ritual, she wasn't a sloven,

She said, 'Cauldron's outdated,

A sword's over-rated.'

So they dance round a microwave oven!

For a faith and practice whose objectives are to change the world for the better and discover the deep hidden powers within each person to the benefit of the whole planet there also has to be harmony, laughter and love between people and their divine, eternal parents. The path of witchcraft is long and winding, its rewards are not to be hoarded in a bank vault, but reinvested in an ever-expanding magical circle of human, invisible and holy friends. It is a hard journey, from ignorance, through the testing of possibilities and self-doubt, to eventual acceptance of magical abilities, super senses and a longing to become the best living individual you can be. No one needs to make that journey alone, nor does anyone have to join those who make them feel uncomfortable.

If you ask for guidance, companionship and success these will be offered to you within the circle of the turning year, under the endless heritage of the eternal stars.

END WORD

The ways of witchcraft are becoming ever more widely known, but some paths have taken a different road from that which leads from the heart of Nature to the magical ring of traditional arts and crafts. It is easy to accept rules for rituals, fixed dates for festivals, and bits of book knowledge developed in the last half-century as ancient lore. But there is another way, not better, or more clearly linked to some ancient religion, but which encourages each follower to find her or his own direction through the hidden forest. The range of knowledge which our ancestors shared covered a vast array of natural wisdom and wit, information passed on bit by bit as children grew up within rural households. They would learn the names of birds and animals and the uses of plants at their mothers' knees, and the endless pieces of family history, lore, folk tales, beliefs, superstitions, customs and traditions around the countryside as they grew up. Book learning, which the earliest charmers, folk healers, bone-setters, witches, cunning men and wise women avidly acquired, added to the inheritance of Nature's own instructions, making them truly wise and cunning. Today we are rich in information, but often it is two-dimensional, static and hard to apply in real life; it lacks stimulation of the other senses of smell, touch, taste and hearing. It can be lonely, if it is merely read from a lifeless and limiting machine, without the warmth of human companionship, sharing and debate.

Anyone can follow the secret paths of witchcraft, but many of these are overgrown, lost or destroyed by modern lifestyles and, to urban, twenty-first century people, they may seem alien and difficult. However, they are life-enriching, self-empowering, confidence-boosting and love- and light-enhancing. From long-lost roots in a distant culture, ideas, beliefs, knowledge and learning have continued to seep into our technological world like fresh water from a hidden spring. Anyone can seek out that fountain and drink deeply of that timeless source of witch wisdom, if they so desire.

Marian Green

Somerset

March 2001

GLOSSARY

These are my own definitions, rather than dictionary definitions.

Agape	Greek for a love feast, which developed into a communion meal (pronounced A-gar-pey). This is often part of a festival celebration in which a goblet of wine and some festival bread is shared.
Age of Aquarius	Due to the movement of the Sun compared to the Earth against the stars of the Zodiac (precession), we are entering the Age of Aquarius, when the Sun will be seen to rise in front of the constellation Aquarius at dawn on the Spring equinox, sometime after 2200 CE.
Age of Pisces	At present the Spring equinox Sun rises against the last stars of Pisces, as they have done for about 2,000 years.
Amulet	This is a flat, carved or painted object, often in the shape of an Eye, worn to ward off harm. The name comes from the same root as 'omelette'. (See *Charm, Talisman* and *Spell*.)
Astral travel	Spiritual journeys, often during sleep, when the dreaming self leaves the physical body, sometimes called out-of-body experiences.
Athame	A ritual dagger (pronounced Ath-a-mey) used by *wiccans*, usually with a black handle, inspired by the works of *Gerald Gardner*.

Aura	The coloured patterns of energy around living things, visible to *witches* and magicians. It is made up of two parts, the inner, denser etheric part which most people can see, and the more subtle and continuously varying outer part made up of strands of light.
Beltane	An old bonfire festival at the beginning of May, when the hawthorn flowers, from the Celtic words 'Bel', good or light, and 'tan', fire.
Book of Illumination	A personal record of *spells*, poems, rituals and other useful information collected by the magic worker. Some wiccans have a *Book of Shadows* which contains scripts for rituals and knowledge passed down within a *coven*.
Book of Lives	The Akashic Record, a living archive where details of all a person's lives are recorded throughout time.
Book of Shadows	A book written by each wiccan, copying the rituals and festivals of their particular *coven* or line of *initiation*. (See *Book of Illumination*.)
Chafing dish	This is a flat metal or pottery dish on which incense is burned on charcoal.
Chakra	One of seven energy centres running through the body, down the length of the spine. The name is Sanskrit for 'Wheel' and they are often depicted as many-petalled lotus flowers.
Charm	A magical object, traditionally a natural thing like a *holey stone* or eye-shaped pebble or four-leaved clover, for example, which brings luck or health. Now a term used to charm or enchant (bless) an object for this use.
Common Era	Usually written CE and replaces AD as a dating system.
Conjure	An old art of calling spirits of Nature or the dead to answer questions. Now used to distinguish magic, sometimes spelled magick, from conjuring tricks. Originally an occult art used by *witches*.
Coven	A group of thirteen or less wiccans, who are led by a High Priestess and High Priest, from the same word as

'convent'. It is necessary to undergo an *initiation* into a coven, although there is little historical evidence of such groups existing before the twentieth century.

Crowley, Aleister A magician and writer who died in 1947, whose work with magical orders and poetry and rituals influenced the people who developed wicca, although he was never directly involved.

Deocil Clockwise or 'godwise', the direction the Sun appears to move in the sky.

Discarnate Not alive on Earth; invisible beings like ghosts or angels.

Divination The many arts of consulting 'the divine', for example, reading Tarot cards, Runes, the I Ching, Astrology, *dowsing*, or consulting oracles.

Dowsing From the old Cornish, 'to seek', especially water or buried treasure, using a Y-shaped hazel 'dowsing rod' or a pendulum.

Elementals Spiritual Beings – gnomes for earth, undines for water, salamanders for fire and sylphs for air – who may be called upon for the help of their element, or may be seen by trained *witches* in Nature.

Ephemeris A list of tables of positions of the planets, the Sun and Moon, used by astrologers, astronomers and navigators.

Equinox The time of year when day and night are equal. This occurs in spring and in the fall.

Esbat A meeting of *wiccans*, at the full moon usually, from the old French 'esbattre – to dance.'

Gardner, Gerald One of the people who publicized the idea of 'wica' as a branch of the old religion. In his novel, *High Magic's Aid*, he set out many of the ideas and practices used within *covens* today. He also wrote *The Meaning of Witchcraft* and *Witchcraft Today*. He died in 1965.

Glyph A magical diagram or symbol, the best known of which is the glyph of the Tree of Life of the *Qabalah*.

Golden Dawn	The Hermetic Order of the Golden Dawn, founded in 1886, in England, from which many modern magical impulses have arisen, including the use of the Tarot for divination and pentagrams for protection. Although the original order split up in the 1920s, offshoots continue its work in many parts of the world.
Golden Mean	This is a ratio of 1:1.618 between the lengths of the sides of a rectangle, which produce regular patterns. It occurs in nature in spiral snail shells and flower petals, and the human body.
Hermetic Mysteries	A general name for much of Western Ceremonial Magic. Hermes was the Greek god of wisdom, based on the Egyptian god, Thoth, who gave the understanding of magic to human kind. Mysteries are things which cannot be told, only experienced. It includes dozens of different influences, from Egyptian to Christian, from Arthurian and Celtic to shamanism and native spiritual traditions of Europe and America.
Holy/Holey stones	These are natural stones, sometimes fossil sponges, which have holes right through them. They have been hung up by red wool or ribbon, to bring luck or protect from harm, over cattle sheds and stables for hundreds of years.
Imbolc	A festival in early February (Northern Hemisphere) when sheep lamb, whose name comes from Celtic and means 'in the belly'. Sometimes called 'Oimelc', meaning Ewe's milk. Also called Candlemas or the Feast of St Bridget.
Incantation	A chant to bring about a particular objective. Sometimes spoken in a foreign language or ancient tongue for psychological effect. (See *Spell*.)
Initiation	This is a ceremony which often signifies rebirth into a group or *coven*, using a variety of symbolic acts, like the taking of wiccan names, binding and perhaps scourging, to make the candidate a full member of that

group. There may be further initiations of degrees offered in a similar manner later on. It is an idea borrowed from Ceremonial magical orders or Freemasonry.

Karma   This is another Sanskrit word, meaning fate or balance. Every action accrues spiritual profit or loss, and through a series of lives the balance must be worked out.

Key of Solomon   This is a book from the middle ages which sets out how *talismans* are to be made, which symbols are used, and the basis of some rituals. It shows pictures of various knives, instruments and symbols which have been taken up by *wiccans*.

Lodge   A group of magicians meet in a lodge, as do Freemasons. It is a term used for both the building or temple and the group itself. Most Lodges are led by a female or male Magus or Magian.

Mabon   In Welsh this means 'son' or 'boy' and is another name for the divine child born at midwinter.

Moon Herbs   Plants which are traditionally associated with the Moon, having white flowers, like jasmine, white roses, poppies or morning glory. Old herbals will tell you which planet each plant is atrributed to.

Menses   A woman's 'moon flow' or period.

Paganism   Originally the simple faith of country people, or those not part of the army of Christ. Today, followers of wicca, druidism, natural spirituality and some native traditional faiths use the umbrella term of pagan. Others, especially followers of the Northern tradition of Odinism, call themselves heathens.

Pentacle   A five-sided shape, known geometrically as a 'pentagon', ('penta' is Greek for five), as opposed to a pentagram, which has five points. (A pantacle is a universal talisman, from Greek 'pan' meaning 'all'.)

Psychometry	The art of sensing the history of an object or information about its owner by touch.
Qabalah	One of the three spellings for an ancient Hebrew system of philosophy, wisdom and magic. These are the Jewish Kabbalah, the Christian Cabala and the mystical Qabalah. The variations come from transliterating the Hebrew letters QBL into English.
Querent	In a divination situation the querent is the one asking a question which the diviner is trying to answer.
Rosicrucian tradition	Based on the writings of a secret brotherhood, whose symbol was a rose and a cross, from the 16th-century. A series of rituals, healing arts and magical skills have been handed down. Part was preserved by Freemasons and part by alchemists and magicians. Its roots go back to ancient Egypt.
Sabbat	This is a name for the eight important seasonal festivals of the *wiccans*. It is derived from Sabbath, the holy day of the week.
Shaman	Originally a tribal worker with magic and spirits from Siberia who, having experienced a death-like state, could recall souls or find healing for the sick.
Sidereal	Star time, used by many astrologers as the time frame from which they calculate the positions of the planets and stars in a horoscope. It differs slightly from 'clock' time.
Skyclad	Some wiccans work their rituals naked or 'skyclad', although this means they often have to meet indoors. Historically, the only people to perform ritual naked were the early Christians, in their ceremonies of baptism.
Solstice	At midsummer and midwinter the Sun reaches the highest and lowest points of its cycle, giving each hemisphere of the world its longest and shortest days.
Speculum	A speculum is any kind of gazing glass or scrying bowl, like a crystal ball, bowl of water or black mirror. It is used to see into the future or at a distance.

Spell	Magical words, chanted, sung or spoken, may be written down and used as a *charm*. *Incantation* is the art of repeating spells.
Sunwise	Clockwise. It is usual to walk circles clockwise, sunwise, or *deocil* to open a ritual space, and close by walking counter-clockwise.
Talisman	This is a deliberately-made object which draws on the power and symbols of the planets or signs of the zodiac, often using archaic writing, to bring about a single specific purpose.
Thurible	An incense burner, often on chains so it can be swung to cense a ritual space. These are often used in churches, or carried in processions.
Tree of Life	This is a diagram or glyph, consisting of ten spheres connected by twenty-two paths, showing the spiritual evolution of creation. It is central to the *Qabalah*, and is used by many Western magicians as a kind of road map, showing where planetary or angelic powers may be located.
Valiente, Doreen	She was in many ways the Mother of Wicca, although she never referred to herself other than as a *witch*. Her prayer, 'The Charge of the Goddess', and the forms and words of many wiccan rituals were hers, begun when she worked with *Gerald Gardner*, but continued independently until her death in 1999.
Warlock	A term from the Anglo-Saxon 'waerloga', a lie teller or deceiver, sometimes mistakenly used as a word for a male *witch*.
Wiccans	Wiccans are initiated into the modern form of *coven witchcraft*, where they are led by a High Priestess and High Priest in their seasonal rituals. They are *pagans* in belief, but tend to use magic less than *witches*. Most of their rituals and practices have been developed since the middle of the twentieth century.

Widdershins	Counter-clockwise, from a Scottish dialect word. The Earth actually turns this way, making the Sun appear to move clockwise. Circles are walked widdershins to close down the power at the end of a ritual.
Witch	A male or female person who uses the powers of Nature to work magic for healing or guidance. May use ritual and celebrate the passing seasons but is not necessarily a pagan, rather one who follows a personal nature spirituality in order to work spells with power.
Witchcraft	The many traditional skills of magic, *charms*, *spells*, healing, *divination*, far-seeing and seasonal ceremony, which are used by *witches*.
Yule	This is the old Norse word, written 'Jul', and meaning 'wheel' for the time around the midwinter solstice. Celebrations include burning a Yule log to strengthen the power of the reborn sun.
Zener cards	Special cards with clear shapes of a circle, square, cross, star and wavy lines, used to test Extra Sensory Perception or psychic power.

BOOK LIST

This is a short list of books, many of whose authors have written several other titles. Also, each of the publishers mentioned will have produced many other titles on related subjects.

Rae Beth *Hedge Witch* Hale, London 1990.

Lois Bourne *Conversations With a Witch* Hale, London 1989.

Vivianne Crowley *Living as a Pagan in the Twenty-first Century* Aquarian, London 1989.

Vivianne Crowley *The Principles of Wicca* Thorsons, London 1999.

Patricia Crowther *Lid Off the Cauldron* Muller, London 1981.

Janet and Stewart Farrar *Eight Sabbats for Witches* Hale, London 1981.

Gerald B Gardner *The Meaning of Witchcraft* Aquarian, London 1959.

Gerald B Gardner *Witchcraft Today* Rider, London 1954.

Marian Green *A Witch Alone* Thorsons, London 1991.

Marian Green *Practical Magic* Lorenz Books, London 2001.

Marian Green *The Gentle Arts of Natural Magic* Thoth Publications, Loughborough, reprinted 1997.

Marian Green *The Path Through the Labyrinth* Thoth Publications, Loughborough, reprinted 1997.

Dr Graham Harvey (editor) *Listening People, Speaking Earth* Hurst, London 1997.

Ronald Hutton *Triumph of the Moon* Oxford University Press, Oxford 2000.

Ronald Hutton *Stations of the Sun* Oxford University Press, Oxford 1996.

Ronald Hutton *Pagan Traditions of the Ancient British Isles* Oxford University Press, Oxford 1991.

John Evan Jones and Doreen Valiente *Witchcraft – A Tradition Renewed* Hale, London 1990.

Charles Leland *Aradia, The Gospel of Witches* David Nutt, London 1899.

Doreen Valiente *Natural Magic* Hale, London 1975.

Doreen Valiente *The ABC of Witchcraft* Hale, London 1973.

Doreen Valiente *The Charge of the Goddess* Hexagon Hoopix, Eastbourne 2000.

Doreen Valiente *Witchcraft for Tomorrow* Hale, London 1978.

USEFUL ADDRESSES

Marian Green may be contacted via the Publishers or at Marian Green, BCM–SCL Quest, London WC1N 3XX, UK, for details of her latest publications and for workshop information.

The Pagan Federation, BM Box 7097, London WC1N 3XX, UK offers membership, conferences, local meetings and other information.

Circle Sanctuary, PO Box 219, Mount Horeb, WI 53572, for news and contacts in the USA.